UNATTACHED

Essays on Singlehood

Angelica Malin

SQUARE PEG

1 3 5 7 9 10 8 6 4 2

Square Peg, an imprint of Vintage,
One Embassy Gardens, Nine Elms, London SW11 7AY

Square Peg is part of the Penguin Random House group of companies
whose addresses can be found at global.penguinrandomhouse.com

Copyright of the Editor © Angelica Malin 2022

Text copyright © Angelica Malin, Annie Lord, Ashley James, Bella DePaulo, Chanté Joseph, Charlie Craggs, Chloe Pierre, Felicity Morse, Francesca Specter, Jessica Morgan, Ketaki Chowkhani, Lucie Brownlee, Madeleine Spencer, Megan Barton-Hanson, Mia Levitin, Natalie Byrne, Nicola Slawson, Poorna Bell, Rachel Thompson, Rahel Aklilu, Rebecca Reid, Rose Stokes, Rosie Wilby, Salma El-Wardany, Shani Silver, Shaparak Khorsandi, Shon Faye, Sophia Leonie, Sophia Money-Coutts, Stephanie Yeboah, Venus Libido 2022

Angelica Malin has asserted her right to be identified as the Editor of this Work in accordance with the Copyright, Designs and Patents Act 1988

First published by Square Peg in 2022

Penguin.co.uk/vintage

A CIP catalogue record for this book is available from the British Library

ISBN 9781529110395

Typeset in 11.25/15pt Sabon by Jouve (UK), Milton Keynes
Printed and bound in Great Britain by Clays Ltd, Elcograf S.p.A.

The authorised representative in the EEA is Penguin Random House Ireland,
Morrison Chambers, 32 Nassau Street, Dublin D02 YH68

Penguin Random House is committed to a sustainable future
for our business, our readers and our planet. This book is made
from Forest Stewardship Council® certified paper.

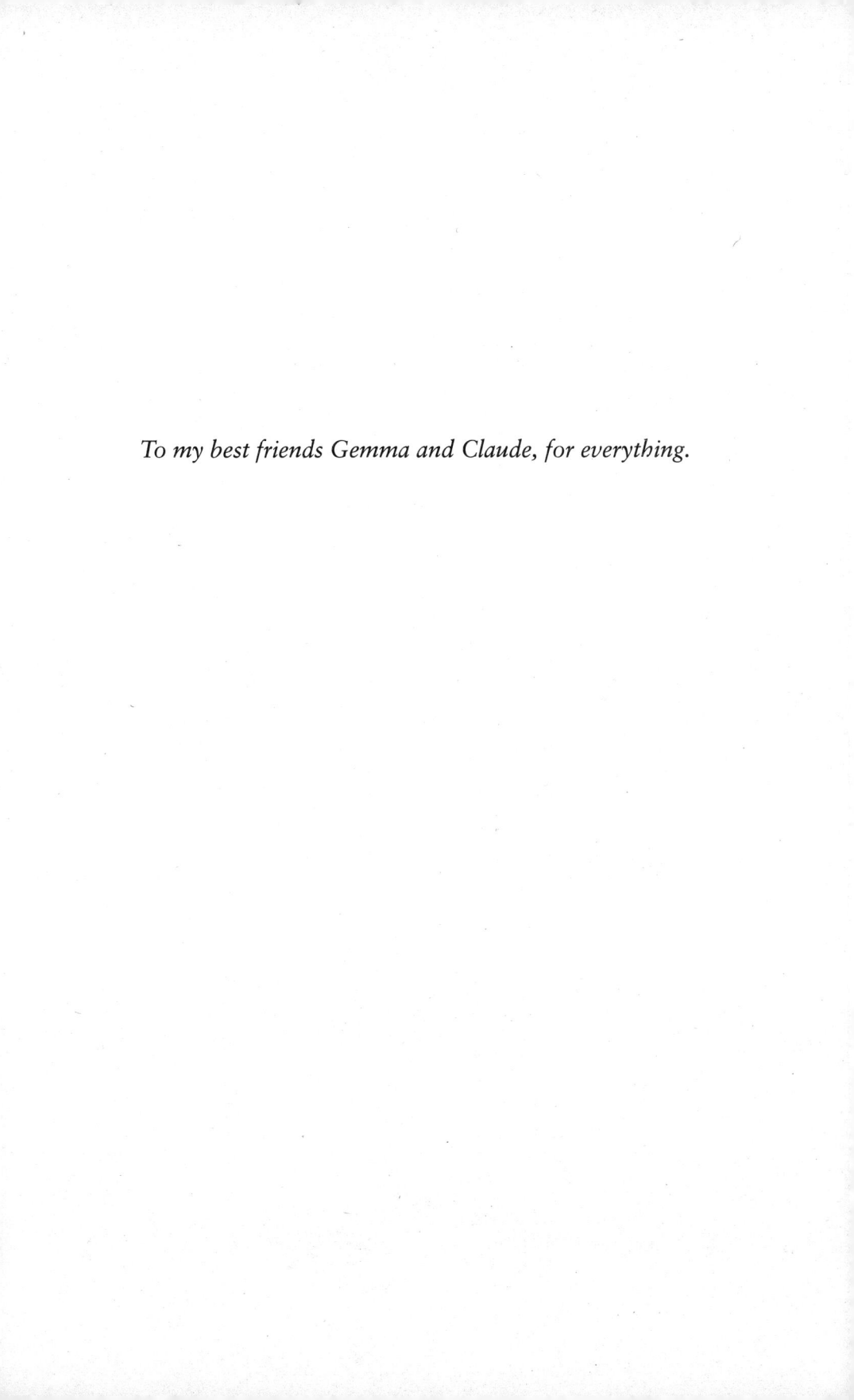

To my best friends Gemma and Claude, for everything.

Contents

Introduction from Angelica Malin — 1

What's in a Peach? — 7
Annie Lord

Better Off Alone (Than with the Wrong Person) — 11
Ashley James

I Always Loved Being Single. The Challenge Was to
   Realise I Always Would — 16
Bella DePaulo

The Joy of Romantic Friendships — 22
Chanté Joseph

Big Macs and Big Dicks — 26
Charlie Craggs

Does Single Womanhood Bother Me? — 30
Chloe Pierre

Writing Your Own Story — 36
Felicity Morse

For Every Single Woman Who's Ever Been Told
   She's the Problem – It's Not You — 41
Francesca Specter

Eat, Pray, Run *Jessica Morgan*	49
Singlehood Unlimited: Solo Living in South India *Ketaki Chowkhani*	54
The Decade Challenge *Lucie Brownlee*	59
Sunday *Madeleine Spencer*	63
Unapologetically Unattached *Megan Barton-Hanson*	67
Dismantling the Dreamhouse *Mia Levitin*	71
Finding Yourself Again + *Amor Fati* *Natalie Byrne*	75
Navigating the Seasons of Friendships as a Single Woman *Nicola Slawson*	81
Soulmates *Poorna Bell*	86
Choosing Myself *Rachel Thompson*	91
Hot Girl Summer *Rahel Aklilu*	96
I'm a Little Bit Jealous of My Single Friends *Rebecca Reid*	100

There Is Nothing to Fear *Rose Stokes*	104
The Golden Days *Rosie Wilby*	109
A Single Woman Is the Closest Living Thing to a Goddess *Salma El-Wardany*	113
The Hamster Wheel *Shani Silver*	118
Stepping Off the Rollercoaster *Shaparak Khorsandi*	122
One Year Without Sex, Love or Dating *Shon Faye*	127
Why All Women Deserve to Experience Being Single in Their Thirties *Sophia Leonie*	133
Empowering, Not Embarrassing: Why Egg-Freezing Shouldn't Feel Shameful *Sophia Money-Coutts*	137
The Journey of Being Plus-Size and Single *Stephanie Yeboah*	141
Me, Myself and My Toys *Venus Libido*	146
References	151
About the Editor	153
About the Contributors	155
Acknowledgements	165

Trigger warning

Before we begin, we want to inform you that in this collection of essays, some writers discuss sensitive topics such as domestic violence, abuse, bereavement and grief. This collection also brings up themes such as transphobia, homophobia, racism and discrimination.

If at any point, this book is triggering or upsetting, consider taking a break from reading, skipping the essay or stopping reading. Practice self-care before, during and after reading.

Introduction
Take Your Broken Heart and Turn It into Art

ANGELICA MALIN

On Thursday 19 December 2019, at around 11 p.m., my heart shattered.

A wreckage of a life before this time lay all around me. For months I was unable to inhale without feeling a deep pain in my chest, right under the ribs.

My world flipped on its axis; date nights were replaced with late-night bowls of Apricot Wheats, my camera roll became a barrage of crying selfies, an imagined future disappeared overnight. I was sleepwalking through life, making two cups of builders' tea, not one – months after, there was always a cup of tea, in his favourite turquoise mug, slowly cooling on the countertop.

Weekends, once a thing of pleasure, mini-breaks and Netflix marathons, inherited a new sense of dread. Reaching a weekend used to feel triumphant; now it was characterised by a feeling of failure. Dread loomed over my week – the vastness of space, which we once occupied with ease, now hung over me. I could see my whole life stretching out in front of me – expansive, limitless, free – and it terrified me.

An artificial Christmas tree, which I'd bought in the days before the break-up, to mark our fifth Christmas together, sat in the corner of my living room, taunting me with its fake white snow and glittering fairy lights. The tree had been a symbol of compromise – bringing some festive cheer into a traditional Jewish home – and now it looked on, judging.

The tree stayed until March 2020, at which point the world flipped again, as we plunged into a global lockdown and life as we knew it ended. All my friends, in their respective couples, raced to sit down like a mad game of Musical Chairs and I was very, very alone.

The consolation prizes of being newly single disappeared overnight. Gone were the chances of dating, the distractions of the big city, the opportunity to make questionable life choices.

It's easy to look at your suffering after the fact, in the rear-view mirror after the immediacy of heartache has faded, and say, 'God, that made me strong.' But at the time, you don't feel like that. At the time, you find yourself googling 'Can I die of a broken heart?' at 3 a.m. and crying into a T-shirt that smells faintly of aftershave.

The pain feels raw and exposed – you'll do literally anything to take it away. But what I've learned, from the eighteen months of government-imposed isolation, is there's no way to go around pain – you have to go through it. Right to the centre. Right to the beating heart of it.

And when you come out the other side, you are a different person. Yes, you're stronger, of course. But you're also more self-compassionate. More capable of soothing yourself. More empathic to the world around you and its suffering. More grateful for every day.

You're someone who has looked into the face of the thing you feared the most, took a deep breath and carried on. You are becoming a version of yourself that you never thought possible – and you may never have got there without the pain.

This book would have never existed if it wasn't for that heartbreak.

I couldn't see that at the time, but our story is always unfolding in mysterious ways. Everyone has their own *Sliding Doors* moment, and what I've learned is that you have to trust – wildly, blindly – that things are unfurling exactly as they are meant to. Things aren't happening *to* you, they are happening *for* you.

In the months that followed, as the pandemic raged on, I started to see life differently. I luxuriated in late-night work sessions without feeling guilty, mid-morning bubble baths, weekends full of self-care – I started unfurling from a couple and rediscovering myself. We don't realise at the time the extent to which we're shaped and constrained by another person; I was no longer defined by the other, but was a person in my own right. One who survived a pandemic, living alone, with a *Monstera* plant called Charlie for company.

When you emerge from a relationship, you rediscover parts of yourself that feel long forgotten, like embracing an old friend. Slowly you start to see the shape of yourself as a whole person – not one who's half of a pair. Your tastes, your personal goals, your latent desires, they begin to emerge again. It's easy to forget these things, when you're working so hard to fit perfectly into half of a whole. I don't blame you – the journey of discovering yourself is not made easy by the world we live in. The world is simpler in a couple; M&S meal deals, two-for-one cinema tickets, Valentine's Day set menus – you're more digestible and commercially viable to the world when you're in a couple.

In many ways, I think we fear a single woman. She's powerful, self-assured and independent. The world wants women who are insecure and self-conscious, because they are easier to sell to. Should we fear being single – or does the world just make us fear it, because a single woman is a force to be feared? By diverting from the narrative that you need to be coupled up to be happy, you are literally turning a commercial model on its head.

But there's more to life than finding 'the one'.

Which is why I wanted to edit this book. To tell a different story – one that's about expansion and possibility, about living fully and deeply. I wanted to bring together a tribe of women who have discovered a secret new world – and a deeper level of consciousness – which only happens when you choose to see singlehood as empowering, not depressing.

This book brings together the voices and experiences of thirty women who will show you that there's not one way to be happy. Life can really open up when you're single – and the path to fulfilment isn't the same for everyone.

Unattached is the work of twelve months, but also the work of a lifetime. It has taken me thirty years to understand and truly believe that I can be happy alone. That, sometimes, the things you sacrifice by being in a relationship – freedom, your Saturday nights, un-merged friendship groups – aren't always worth it. And the things you gain by being alone – independence, spontaneous travel, being brilliantly selfish, eating Marmite on toast for dinner – are to be celebrated.

There's so much to be gained by being single. From discovering who you really are, to creating deep friendships on your own terms, being single allows you to shape and mould your life in a way that suits you – without bending to the will of another. It allows you to know yourself – and, thereby, know what you really want in a relationship (if at all). As you'll discover in this book, often by cultivating a compassionate, loving relationship with yourself, the by-product is often a better relationship with a romantic partner.

Being single makes you strong.

When you're constantly looking for validation and reassurance from another person, you need them to prop you up. You'll look for someone to tell you that you can achieve anything – and without that validation, you fear you can't succeed. I don't need that any more. When someone says to me, 'I believe in you', I say, 'That's sweet, but I don't need you to believe in me, because I believe in me.' Because I have learned to support myself, to hold my own hand through life.

When you take away the option of leaning on another, you start to lean into yourself – to hear yourself clearly and connect with your own intuition. At least the decisions you make are guided by you – and you alone. And the responsibility is yours, too. What a gift that is: to know that everything you need in life is within you. And that it always was – but needs its opportunity to shine through.

You don't have to wait to build the life you want. The following October I got a little Cavapoochon puppy called Alfie. It was the first major life decision I'd made out of a relationship for

Introduction

years – and it was the best thing I ever did. This little puppy showed me limitless love; he rested his head on my chest in the evening, stole my place in the bed overnight and licked my feet good morning. He is a daily reminder that there are different kinds of love and fulfilment in this life – and romantic love isn't the only one that matters. If we stopped, just for a moment, obsessing over romantic love – as beautiful as it is – and created a little more space to see the world around us, our friendships, our family and the beauty in the everyday, I think we'd all be happier.

If you're picking up this book and you're feeling sad and alone, I want to tell you that it's all going to be OK.

One day you're going to be so strong and brave, and you'll go on solo weekends away and eat dinner in a fancy restaurant on your own and spend evenings with your girlfriends, and it will nourish you so deeply, so fully. And it's also perfectly fine if you're not there yet, but don't rush this time. Don't wish away your single years to keep up with a generation of Instagram brides and cookie-cutter timelines. Being single is an ebb and flow, sometimes hard, sometimes easy, but don't fritter away the time worrying about the future; just go through it with your eyes open – and revel in the specialness of it.

There's so much growing, learning and self-discovery to do in life – and you'll learn more about yourself being single than you ever will in a relationship. I want that for you. I want you to wake up and seize all of life's opportunities without worrying that you need a partner to do something. I want you to live unapologetically. I want you to walk into a room, the most confident person there, without needing a man to tell you that you look great. I want you to fly to Rome, sit in a pavement café and drink coffee whilst people-watching, without ever feeling self-conscious that you're without a partner to accompany you. Because you are more than enough on your own. You always were. You always will be. Don't let the world make you think otherwise.

What's in a Peach?

ANNIE LORD

I'm pretty lazy when it comes to food. A lot of the time I have cereal for dinner. I don't cook anything that requires any more than two steps, which means almost everything I make is a traybake. I get impatient with vegetables and take them out of the oven when they're still crunchy in the middle. I heat everything at 200°C because, most of the time, that's vaguely the right temperature. I batch-cook huge amounts of food, which often ends up with me having to eat the same fucked-up lunch and dinner for days on end – think Thai Green Curry that ended up brown for some reason, or a stir-fry where all you can taste is burn. I never buy fresh herbs. I use puréed garlic, so I don't have to chop anything. There's never much washing-up to do.

I wasn't always like this. When I was in a relationship I took much more time over food, because what my ex put in his mouth felt important. There would be harissa-flavoured yoghurt to drizzle over chicken, spice pastes, dry rubs with sugar and cayenne pepper. If I went to Sainsbury's and they didn't have okra, I would walk the extra fifteen minutes to the market to get it. I'm not saying I was a talented cook. I once accidentally evaporated all the soup from the ramen I was making, so it ended up as noodles and overcooked chicken; there were aubergines that came out as dry as cardboard, chewy steaks, but the point is, I always tried. He'd come in from work and flop on the sofa and I'd ask, 'Is it nice? It's grim, isn't it? Is it all right?' until he complimented me; and I'd enjoy watching the way he'd bend his head down over the food, shovelling another forkful in before he'd even swallowed the first bit, leaning back on the sofa and breathing out, hand on stomach. I liked the feeling of filling him all the way up.

Food is one of the best ways of saying, 'I love you.' My mum likes Lindor chocolates, and my dad buys her so many of them for her that their red boxes sit on the kitchen counter because there's not enough room for them in the cupboards, almost as if he's saying: this is how much I never want you to need anything. When my brother and I visit home, Dad makes us bacon sandwiches and brings them up to us in bed as though it's code for: you'll never know how much I missed you.

I took time with my food before, not because I loved myself, but because I loved someone else. When he left, I stopped bothering with my cooking as much. I burned toast, scraped off the black bits and ate the rest, even if it didn't taste very good. Now I never use more than one pot.

When women fall in love with men, they can forget themselves in that other body. It's not hard to work out why this happens. So much of the world is holding us back all the time; we're interrupted when we're speaking, credit is taken for the work we do, and then we meet this other person who never encounters any of the same roadblocks. We can seek to transpose ourselves into these freer brings, thinking we'll be free if we can live through them. We curate the conditions so they can flourish. Whether saying, 'No, it's fine, I was nearly done anyway' when you're reading and they want to turn off the bedroom light, or beginning far too many sentences with 'My boyfriend says . . .', we sometimes disappear so much into them that it stops mattering how we feel and becomes all about how they feel.

Since my partner and I broke up, I've had to learn how to find that other part of myself again in so many big ways. I'm doing well at work. I have new friends. I went on holiday. I moved house. Accept that you don't exist only during those life-changing moments, but also in every small 'Should I get the bus or should I walk?', 'Should I light that candle or should I save it?', 'Should I find a new recipe or should I make that pasta I always make?'

My ex taught me this. We were leaving the cinema and I was jealous because an ex-girlfriend, whom he had previously gone travelling with, messaged him asking how he was.

'You guys went to Indonesia and saw volcanoes and sunsets,' I said, moaning. 'With me, you just get emptying out the bins and the Odeon.'

'But that's real life, isn't it?' he replied, rubbing my arm. 'Making it work is the most romantic thing in the world.'

He was right. Love isn't all about getting down on one knee or sprinkling the bed in rose petals. It's about giving them your last chip, letting them rest their head on your arm even though the weight makes it go dead, listening to them moan about their boss – without coming up with any solutions; just listening; writing something down on your phone that you know they will find funny, so you don't forget to tell them about it when you see them later; being nice to their friend that you hate, simply because you know they like them; staying on the phone with them even when you have stuff to do; not getting annoyed when they say they don't want a dessert and then eat yours; letting go the fact that they didn't sweep the floor when they said they would sweep the floor. It's funny because I can do so many of these nice things I did for him, for myself. It would probably make me a lot happier. I might not even want a boyfriend. I just never do them, because I'm not sure if I deserve them. It's funny because so many of these things I can do for myself – if only I thought myself worthy of receiving them.

One Monday it's sunnier than usual, and I'm not sure what it is – maybe it's the sweet spot in my menstrual cycle when my hormones are perfectly balanced, maybe it's the sun leaking out the side of the spring clouds – but I act in a way that I don't usually. I finish work early to go on a walk because I can and, on my way, I stop at a fruit stall. I have loads of leftover pesto chicken from a few nights ago at home that I was meant to eat for dinner, but I'm not in the mood for it. I decide I'm going to make something else, and the dizziness of breaking a habit and knowing I have other options makes me prickle with excitement. It's like when you're a kid and your mum says, 'Off you go; just make sure you're back before it gets dark.' At the fruit stall there are all these peaches, which have reached that perfect ripeness where the dusty red skin fades into a deep mustard yellow, the most colourful of sunsets. I buy too many of them and all the ingredients to make a pie.

At home, I move a knife through the furry skin and the juice dribbles stickiness down my wrists. I think about the evening that stretches out in front of me and imagine spending it reading the book I've had on my shelf for far too long. I line a pan with butter and then roll out the puff pastry into it. Instead of putting a podcast on, I enjoy the quiet, occasionally speckled with the faint sound of sirens and cars whooshing past the window. I spread ricotta and vanilla syrup onto the base and I think about the embarrassing thing I said when I was last drunk and how, maybe, it wasn't that embarrassing. I put it in at 210°C, like the recipe says, and remember a nice encounter I had with an old man who needed directions and, instead of explaining, I walked him there instead.

When the pie is ready, I cut a too-big slice that is all tarry and sticky on top, because I'm pretty sure God got something wrong when he said that gluttony was one of the seven deadly sins. I get back into bed with a plateful and, with my fork, I scoop up all that sour sugariness until there's nothing left except the flakes of pastry that I press onto my fingers and into my mouth. And, though the recipe wasn't so confusing that I needed to ring my dad and ask for help, though it didn't require me to marinate something for twenty-four hours, nor did I need to squeeze anything out of a piping bag, it meant the same. It meant, 'I love you.' I said the words aloud to myself, and I meant it.

Better Off Alone (Than with the Wrong Person)

ASHLEY JAMES

'I've got so much love to give and no one to give it to,' I sobbed into a wet tissue.

I had just been dumped, again. I say dumped, but I'm not sure you can really be dumped if you never even made it to the official stage. Equally, I don't know that being ghosted even counts as dumped?

'I'm nearly thirty,' I cried. 'All the nice ones are gone, and I'm going to be alone for ever!'

I'd been on the single side of dating for almost four years – and not through choice, I might add. My last relationship had ended very badly, and I felt utterly unlovable for a long time afterwards. The more I chased love, the more it seemed to evade and elude me. To make matters worse, I was running out of time (or so I thought).

That was three years ago; I was to remain single for another two, and the man I was crying over was one of the very many emotionally unavailable guys who broke my heart during my 'early' single years. I make the distinction between the early and the later years because my thoughts, feelings, habits and behaviours in the two phases were worlds apart. Unrecognisable, almost. And that is what led me out of my misery and into a life filled with more love than I could ever imagine back then. But more on that later.

Let's rewind to me snivelling into a tissue over that totally unsuitable guy I'd convinced myself I was in love with. I was completely broken-hearted. But, in all honesty, it wasn't wholly his fault. In truth, I never gave myself a chance to heal fully from the heartbreak I'd experienced before that. I thought I could only be mended by the man I pined for choosing to love me back.

The problem was, I kept going after people who weren't right for me. If a guy told me he wasn't looking for a relationship, that would be my cue to pursue him obsessively and compulsively. My brain would go into overdrive as I set myself up for the challenge. I would imagine our future together, tell myself that he would eventually see my worth if only I proved it to him, and that I would miraculously change him. Inevitably, and probably unsurprisingly, I was left in tatters each and every time.

I wasn't a total masochist, hell-bent on my own suffering – rather, the men I dated were aptly skilled at knowing exactly how much hope to give me, to keep me hanging around. There was always a nugget of affection for me to cling onto; they would tell me they had never felt like this before, but there was always a reason why they couldn't be with me – for instance, they were still messed up from a previous relationship, had a crazy ex that haunted them (*huge* red flag!), a difficult upbringing that prevented them from settling down, or were just not in the right 'headspace', for one reason or another: focusing on their work was a commonly occurring excuse. No matter the problem, I convinced myself that I was the solution – and that I could fix this thing.

As I whimpered into my Kleenex for that final time, I realised something had to change. I had spent so long trying to heal the wounding, and improve other people, that I had neglected to look after myself. One thing I knew for sure was that it was time to stop putting my self-esteem in the hands of others, letting them build me up and knock me down, as and when they pleased. I realised in that moment that the only person I could really rely on to make me happy was myself. It was time to go inwards.

So I did what any heartbroken romantic would do and booked a one-way ticket to a far-away destination. Mexico was my choice of medicine. I'll admit that at the time, though, soul-searching wasn't my only objective. I set off to find myself, but I did secretly hope that I might find 'the one' on my travels, too.

Of course that didn't happen (I had much work to do before it could). But the fact that this fantasy even crossed my mind exemplifies quite how desperate I was to meet someone – anyone. I was a hopeless romantic. In fact I referred to myself as such, with pride. Though I realise now that I'm not completely to blame. I was brought up on Disney films and rom-coms, and even as a thirty-year-old feminist with a successful career and my own home, I was still playing the damsel in distress, waiting for someone to come along and 'save me'. From what? That is the question.

Arriving in Mexico, I was so very alone, but there was something about being by myself on the other side of the world that I also found to be completely liberating. I was free to travel and hang out with whomever I wanted. I felt the sand in my toes, the salty breeze on my skin, watched incredible sunsets and went wherever the wind took me. It dawned on me that my friends who were in relationships or had families of their own didn't have this kind of freedom. They had to plan, discuss, debate, find a time that worked for both parties, and maybe even compromise on the destination they dreamed of. I, on the other hand, could do anything I pleased.

No better was this illustrated to me than one night in a pizza place on Holbox Island. The restaurant was in no way fancy, but as I watched the sky turn to pink and then orange, I thought how nice it would be to share this moment with a significant other. I looked around to find that I was surrounded by couples – a sea of people who had the very thing I craved. Only they weren't being present and enjoying the moment that I hoped and dreamed of so badly. Instead they were staring into their phones, barely paying attention to each other, let alone the beautiful sunset. I sat there, fantasising about being next to someone I'd never even met, yet the couples around me were in paradise with their partners and they didn't even seem to notice. It dawned on me that although I was the one who was alone, they seemed lonelier.

It made me think of how much of my life I had put on hold for a total stranger, for 'the one', for a person I didn't even know existed yet. For a moment I thought, 'What if I choked on my pizza right now and didn't make it to the Maldives?' I had wanted to save the trip for my dream honeymoon and it suddenly made me laugh out loud, because I didn't even really want to get married at this point. And what if I met someone who hated the sun? Or had a phobia of flying? Or what if he was already in the Maldives? Where exactly did I think this person was waiting for me? At home? Surely I was more likely to meet that ever-elusive 'one' if I started really living the life I wanted to live? It also pushed me to think about all of the love that I already had in my life. Amazing friends and a supportive family. I wondered how perhaps those relationships might be even richer if I stopped directing all of my energy and focus into someone who, at this point, was nothing more than a figment of my imagination.

Although I returned from Mexico still single, I did come back with a newfound love: for myself, and for those around me. I made a promise to start investing my love, care and attention into nourishing myself, and nurturing my relationships. I booked that trip to the Maldives that I had always saved for a romantic partner, with my best friend instead. We went diving, we drank wine, we saw sunrises and sunsets and we made memories. My heart was full.

And so comes the moral of the story. Romantic love is wonderful, but it's not the only kind. There is so much love to be found in the world, and if you open your eyes wide enough, you'll notice that you're already surrounded by it. Not to mention that when you're going through a period of singleness, it's all too easy to forget that not every relationship is a happy one, and sometimes you really are better off alone. Once you learn that you can live the life you want to by yourself, and on your own terms, you don't want to settle for anyone just to fill a void. As journalist and author Elizabeth Gilbert wisely said:

> At some point we all have to learn how to walk into a party or a restaurant alone. Otherwise, we will be willing to walk in with ANYBODY (or worse, walk out with anybody). We have to learn how to endure our own company and hold our heads high. And sometimes, after enough time alone, we might even learn to enjoy ourselves.

I have so much love to give and so many people to give it to: my family, my friends, my dog and, most importantly, me. I learned to love myself enough that I stopped giving my time to people who didn't deserve it. And eventually I met someone who did. Not through trying, not by pushing, not by forcing, but by simply surrendering and allowing love to find me.

I've just booked to go back to Mexico with my love and our son. A lot of my friends who were in relationships then are now single. So when you feel like you're being left behind, remember: life is not a race. Being in a relationship is not a sign of happiness or success, nor is it always for ever. My biggest superpower is knowing that I am perfectly complete when alone. It can be yours, too – if you want it to be.

I Always Loved Being Single. The Challenge Was to Realise I Always Would

BELLA DEPAULO

On 17 December 1992 I clipped an advice column from a local newspaper and slipped it into a new folder labelled '1'. I had underlined one sentence: 'Remember that one is a whole number.'

I was thirty-nine, I had been single my whole life and I wasn't looking for reassurance. I never felt like I wasn't a whole person because I was single. I just thought it was curious that single life was so often framed as a lesser life, a mere step along the way to a settled coupled life. That clipping launched my study of the psychology of living single.

I never yearned to be married or even have a committed romantic relationship. I had a few boyfriends in high school and college. I understood that looking for a romantic partner was what I was supposed to do. It wasn't terrible. I have no dating horror stories. I kind of liked each of those guys. But each time a relationship ended, I was so very happy to return to my one true love: my single life.

For far too long I didn't know that single life was my one true love, and always would be. I saw my friends and relatives felled by romance, one after another, and I figured that I, too, would be smitten eventually. I thought I was just slow in getting there. I didn't know there was such a thing as loving being single and wanting to stay single for life.

Looking back, all the signs were there. I simply missed every last one of them. I kept waiting for my desires and my life to start unfolding like everyone else's. It is now my life's work, my mission and my passion, to make it known that for untold numbers of people, single life is our best, most authentic, most meaningful and most fulfilling life. I call us 'single at heart'. We are not single because we have 'issues', because we were unlucky in love, because we haven't found the right person or because we are so sick of the chase, we've given up. Single is who we authentically are.

We also don't believe that being single is better than being in a bad romantic relationship, or that it is better to be single than to wish you were. Those sentiments are far too grudging. For us, no life is better than single life.

I'm a social psychologist, but my understanding of people who are single at heart does not come from the work of my fellow social scientists. Most of the researchers who included single people in their studies were really interested in marriage or romantic relationships. They seemed sure that married life was the superior life, and they designed and interpreted their research in ways that were biased to show just that. The single people were foils. Until very recently, hardly anyone bothered to ask single people if they wanted to be single. Maybe they couldn't imagine that anyone did.

I imagined it, I lived it and I asked about it. On Valentine's Day in 2012 I posted online a brief quiz I had created, 'Are You Single at Heart?' By 2019, when I was ready to analyse the data, more than 8,000 people from more than 100 countries had responded. Another forty-two people who identified as single at heart shared their life stories with me, answering dozens of personal questions, often in great detail. Because of their openness and generosity, I can tell you about my own single-at-heart life in a more valuable way. I have a better idea of which of my experiences were signs that single life was the best life for me, and which were merely idiosyncratic.

The signs

Romantic partners are never going to take centre-stage in our lives
I knew that not being in a romantic relationship was supposed to hurt. My older brother had already got married. So had my best friend from graduate school and my closest colleague at my first

university job. Now it was my younger brother's turn. But the thing is, I had never felt pained by another person's wedding. A stereotype of single women is that we are bitter, but it is hard to feel bitter about not getting something you never really wanted.

Just like my relief at the ending of romantic relationships that were not terrible, my utter lack of envy of people who got married was probably a sign that I was single at heart. I didn't ask about envy in the 'Single at Heart' quiz, but I did ask about the emotions that people experienced if they were in a romantic relationship and it ended. Of those who identified as definitely single at heart, 84 per cent said they felt relieved and happy to be their own person again. Of those who were definitely not single at heart, 88 per cent instead said they felt mostly sadness and pain.

I wasn't all that interested in dolls as a kid, but I did have Barbies. My Barbies, though, never had a wedding. Ken made an appearance, but he got summarily kicked to the kerb. I didn't think much of that; he was boring. I also didn't read anything into the biographical details missing from my life story: I never made a list of ideal characteristics of a potential spouse. I never collected bridal magazines or fantasised about my wedding. I was too busy living my full and fulfilling single life.

We savour our solitude

I grew up with two parents and three siblings, but rarely did a day go by when only the six of us were at home. Neighbours knocked on the side door, calling out, 'Yoo-hoo, anyone home?', then let themselves in. Aunts, uncles and cousins gathered around the kitchen table for coffee and dessert. A few relatives joined us fairly regularly for dinner. My troops of friends, and my siblings' friends, were all welcome, too.

I adored living in such a warm-hearted home. My favourite time, though, was Sunday nights. That's when everyone else was most likely to scatter, leaving me to luxuriate in solitude. I rarely did anything interesting. I just loved being completely alone. That would never change.

I didn't realise quite how significant my love of solitude was until I analysed the data from my 'Single at Heart' quiz. One of the questions I asked was, 'When you think about spending time alone, what thought comes to mind first?' For those who identify as single at heart, an astonishing 98 per cent answered 'sweet solitude'. Of those who were clearly not single at heart, 59 per cent chose the other option: 'oh, no, I might be lonely!'

Savouring time to ourselves is our single-at-heart superpower. It protects us from the loneliness that is supposed to be our undoing. It renders impotent all those taunts that are hurled at us: 'You're going to grow old alone!', 'You're going to die alone!' Um, yes – I hope so!

I don't mean that I don't want to have people I love in my life; I hope I will always have that. And I don't know whether I'll care one way or another if there are people around me when I die. What I mean is that I hope I will continue to have the financial and physical means that will allow me to live independently until the day I die. Not everyone who is single at heart lives alone, but we all want to live on our own terms, every day of our lives.

We choose who matters to us

Soon after a new colleague, a single woman, was hired in the university department where I had my first teaching job, she invited me to dinner at her place. I was looking forward to it, until she hinted that she might also invite some guys. I didn't want to be set up. I wanted to get to know her.

You know those friends who are so great to have in your life when they are single, but then bench you once they become romantically enthralled? We who are single at heart are not going to do that. We're not looking past our friends as we talk to them, to see if there is some romantic prospect on the horizon.

To be single at heart is to be free to decide who to welcome into your life, and who to prioritise. Friends, relatives, co-workers, neighbours, teammates, fellow volunteers, mentors, kids – we get to open our arms to as many or as few of these people as we want, without worrying about the romantic partners who think they should always come first.

My long-standing interest in creating the social circle that suited me best, rather than defaulting to the expected and celebrated romantic script, was another sign that single life was my best life, and always would be. It was one of those signs that I missed until I started studying other people who are single at heart and discovered that that's what they wanted, too.

We embrace our single lives, and we love our freedom

When I asked the forty-two single-at-heart people who shared their life stories with me what they liked best about being single, every one of them, in some way or another, mentioned freedom. Within the constraints of our resources, opportunities and privileges, we get to decide for ourselves how to live our lives. Choosing who will matter to us is one example. Choosing what will matter is another.

There is no one set of interests or passions that characterises our lives. We cherish our single lives because we get to pursue the paths that feel most authentic and fulfilling. I love the life of the mind, and writing a different, more affirming story about what it means to be single. Nature, sunshine, good friends and good food all make me very happy. Other people who are single at heart use their freedom to travel, hone their creativity, go on great adventures, leave a lucrative job for work that is more meaningful, have kids and raise them according to their own values, or to be there for the people they love when those people are most in need of care.

In my younger days, when newly betrothed women thrust their ringed finger forward and basked in the squeals of joy that greeted their announcement, I may have tried to play along. Later, I would come to wonder why my own milestones did not merit their own congratulatory squeals. I bought a home, all on my own. I earned a PhD from Harvard. I published my book, *Singled Out: How Singles Are Stereotyped, Stigmatized, and Ignored, and Still Live Happily Ever After*. Weren't all those accomplishments made of sterner stuff than a marriage, which could be dissolved at will and, in the United States, actually would be ended more than 40 per cent of the time?

Really, though, I never compared my single life to coupled life to see which seemed better. All along, I think I knew it in my heart. Single life was the one for me. It just took me a long time to understand that it always would be.

If you take only one thing from what I have said, let it be this: for people who love being single, not having a serious romantic partner does not limit our lives, it throws them wide open. When we do not follow the conventional script for living a life, every other possibility in the world is there to beckon us.

The Joy of Romantic Friendships

CHANTÉ JOSEPH

We've all done it: violently rolled our eyes into the back of our head when inundated with too much couple content, but rarely do we take the time to interrogate those feelings. Are you going green because you desire a relationship? Are you feeling extremely single, or is it something else?

Whenever I envied friends or social-media stars in relationships, it was never about the act of being partnered that burned me – because, let's face it, men are not exactly difficult to attract, and not every relationship is nurturing – it was the idea of having an intimate and close relationship with someone who felt the desire to give you support even when they didn't have to. So often we're taught that the only valid and fulfilling type of intimacy is the one we get from sexual and romantic relationships. As women, we are told to believe that only a man can provide us with deep connections that make us whole and, as a result, many of us are set up to fail. Men enter relationships as if they're working at a job they hate, reaping as many benefits as possible while doing the absolute least. Capitalism ruins the sanctity of interpersonal relationships by making them a resource to exploit instead of a space to re-energise and be nurtured.

I've grown increasingly tired of forcing men into situations wherein they hold some sort of responsibility for my feelings, as I have been almost always let down. When you experience romantic mistreatment – be it negging, love-bombing or withholding – it can harden you. The softness that we all possess is robbed from us when we are continuously met with struggle and manipulation within the safe spaces we hold dear. Prioritising these relationships in a misogynistic society means you're scored on how well you can 'keep' a man, so having few or unsuccessful relationships can feel like a bad character trait. In reality, it is much more complex than that. I found that the men I emotionally invested in were not only terrible partners but terrible friends, too. When someone views you as an object instead of a human with emotional needs, it becomes easy for them to detach from the harm caused. So, slowly, I'm learning to de-centre romantic love from men, and am removing them from the top of the intimacy totem pole. By no means is this an easy task, especially when everything in our society centres around romantic relationships. However, you do this by intentionally unlearning contrived ideas around intimacy and embracing what feels natural and real to you. It starts by better understanding the relationships you hold and how you can nurture them to add more to your life.

The belief that compassionate and intimate relationships only exist between sexual partners is (like most things) a construct. Nineteenth-century Western societies that were once fiercely segregated by gender allowed for same-sex friendships to flourish and take priority. For example, nineteenth-century Britain saw the role of men as the provider, out working, while mothers and daughters stayed at home to cover domestic responsibilities. Women were not to speak to men without a chaperone, and if you seemed desperate for male attention or desire, it was shunned. The intimacy shared in these friendships was far from abnormal; in fact, it was encouraged. It was believed that – for women in particular – having intense and intimate relationships made them better prepared for the life of a wife. However, after getting married off, they often missed the connections that they nurtured with other women. Eventually, as women started joining the workforce, growing financially independent and living whole lives that didn't require marriage, things quickly changed. Nineteenth-century New England saw a rise in 'Boston marriages', where two wealthy and educated women cohabited without the interference of a man. Though some of these relationships were romantic, others weren't. Either way, the idea of women leading meaningful and sustainable lives outside of men was petrifying to them. Same-sex relationships – whether sexual or platonic – were looked down on and seen as amoral. Even intimate acts, be it hugging or sleeping in the same bed, were viewed as inappropriate. By relegating friendship as inferior to romantic relationships, both men and women are duped out of balanced lives where multiple people can meet their various needs.

We need to start finding the intimacy and romance within our platonic friendships; there is so much that can fuel us when we no longer attach all forms of intimacy to sexual relationships.

When I think about romantic friendships, my friend Zainab comes to mind. We FaceTime each other more or less every single day. Sometimes we spend hours in silence while we work or scroll on social media; it is a closeness I've never had with anyone else. Our calls began over lockdown, as we were both in a rush to finish our books. What started as an accountability partnership eventually became my favourite friendship. I would do anything for Zai; she created space for me to be vulnerable and open. Through her company, I've been able to take back the softness I once lost in chasing romantic relationships with men. Similarly with my friend Vanessa, despite not being close at university, we found our way back to each other, never going more than two days without speaking. Vanessa has become a massive part of my growth; I'm learning how to be a better friend and also recognising the value I bring to other people.

At the ripe age of twenty-five, I can confidently say that I have two friends I can call on at any time and have their support. This means more to me than the litany of failed relationships and situationships I have had with men. What makes non-sexual intimate relationships so great is that they don't have the labels and expectations that society places on other relationships. You can map and feel your way through a friendship as you please without turning it into a performance. Nobody is pressuring you into making colossal life choices together, and you don't have to follow rules or timelines. Non-romantic sexual relationships don't come with constantly needing to be tested; the relationship isn't dictated by how much you can endure, which is liberating. Believing that intimacy only existed between partners meant that I withheld in certain areas of my life. I don't think I was as good a friend, daughter or sister as I could be, because something about intimacy did not feel right outside a heterosexual relationship. I wasn't able to tap into that side of me because I'd been socialised to believe that closeness only exists when you have a romantic partner.

Changing my relationship with intimacy has adjusted how I relate to my own family. As an older sister, I'm thinking about how to show my younger siblings love, compassion and intimacy helps them find it in friends and family rather than solely in romantic relationships. This, of course, means showering them with gifts and love, but, most importantly, creating a neutral ground for them to share their feelings, ideas and fears. Through unlearning gendered and hetero-normative perceptions of intimacy, not only do I receive love in a healthy and fulfilling way, but I can give it abundantly also, and that makes life so much sweeter.

Big Macs and Big Dicks

CHARLIE CRAGGS

I'm the only person I know who found lockdown easy. In fairness, though, I had a lot of training for it because I had no friends at school.

I thought when school ended I'd stop being lonely and have loads of friends and boyfriends – I thought wrong. Though I date and have friends now, I don't have anyone I'm that close with, and honestly sometimes I feel more lonely now than I did in school. I think it's because when you're in school you know that, even if what you're going through is shit, you have your whole life ahead of you. But now, ten years on in my twenties, I'm realising this is it: this is my life, and I'm living it.

I hope my friends aren't offended after reading that I still feel lonely and I don't feel that close to anyone, because I have some amazing lifelong friends whom I love dearly, but I don't have a best friend.

Any more.

My best friend, Khadija Saye, was killed in the Grenfell Tower fire. We'd been best friends since nursery and I honestly believe she was more of a soulmate than a friend, because the sisterly bond we shared is something I've not even been close to finding with anyone else; and so the last four years since losing her have been as hard as, if not harder than, school. The loneliness is crippling. I think the loneliness in my social life is intensified by the loneliness in my love life, if I'm honest. I do date, but I've not been in love, so I'm always feeling a bit empty and lonely. The number of times I've cried on the way home from meeting friends or going on dates, because it's reminded me how empty and unconnected I feel. This loneliness, or rather how I've coped with this romantic and platonic loneliness in my life, is what I wanted to talk to you about.

I don't think any of us get anywhere by not being totally honest and authentic. We need to explore our messier, embarrassing, ugly and real sides to help ourselves and help others, and that's what I'm going to give you. I hope you read this as a friend, without judgement, and I hope my messy, honest authenticity encourages you to be just as unapologetically honest and authentic, too. This is what we need, to change things.

So the truth is, I was hooking up a lot before lockdown. Don't get me wrong, despite being raised Catholic and still a practising Christian, I'm very sex-positive and I don't think what I was doing was wrong in a shameful way (luckily, the Catholic guilt passed me). I'm all for having fun and living your best life, but that's the thing – I wasn't living my best life. I'm not ashamed of the sex itself, I'm ashamed of who I was having sex with and why I was having it.

I'm not ashamed because they were bad-looking, or bad people, but because they didn't deserve me or my body. More to the point, I didn't deserve to be putting myself through what I was putting myself through by hooking up with these sleazy guys. I think of my inner child, and the life I want for that sweet child, and this is not it. But I understand why I was doing it.

I think there were a few reasons to be honest – obviously, sex feels good, and there's probably some science to do with the dopamine hit when you're depressed – but in all honesty, I think I was having sex to feel less lonely and to actually feel something. Anything.

I was numb after losing Khadija, for years. Even now. I've been diagnosed with complex PTSD recently, and my behaviour over the last few years makes much more sense to me in retrospect, with that diagnosis in mind. I think I was in shock. I could, and still can, sit and stare at a wall for hours in silence. Even if I'm sitting watching my favourite TV shows and films, I find it almost impossible to concentrate. I'm numb.

My way of fighting this numbness was by doing something that made me feel something, that made me feel alive and present and helped me forget. I think hooking up made me feel this way because I was a very late bloomer sexually – I didn't want to date or have sex pre-transition because I was so uncomfortable in my body; and I'd only just started having sex not long before Grenfell happened, so it was still scary and exciting to me. It took me out of my life, my reality and my grief for a moment. I didn't feel numb while I was doing it, because I felt nervous and the sex itself felt good. But what felt better was feeling like I had some control over my life, in the midst of my depression, when my life had been destroyed by this tragedy I couldn't control.

I don't drink, smoke or do drugs, so sex became my comfort and my coping mechanism. It became my drug and, in a weird way, I think I became a little bit addicted. So when the pandemic hit, I was lost. I obviously stopped hooking up, but considering I was doing it because I was lonely in the first place, to then not be able to fight my loneliness during a very isolated time – aka lockdown (which I lived in on my own, for parts) – was tough.

As tough as it was, though, I'm grateful because I honestly don't think I would have stopped hooking up yet, if it wasn't for lockdown. It was a reset for me, like a detox: a fresh start. I don't think I even realised I had a problem in the midst of it, before lockdown. It's hard to see that you have a problem or bad habits when you're caught up in the cycle of everyday life. I don't know about you, but I'm often on autopilot in my everyday life, and it's only when you're lying in bed unable to sleep at 3 a.m. on a random Tuesday night that you realise you're sleepwalking through life. The one life you get. Sometimes you need to stop and break the cycle to see what you're doing right and wrong, and to gain some clarity and perspective, and that's what lockdown has given me and I'm forever grateful for that.

Now, months in, I'm finding celibacy easy. It feels right, like I'm doing something good for myself, like I'm healing. That's why even though I could have started hooking up, with things opening up now after lockdown, I still haven't, and I don't intend to, either.

I have just gone back to grief counselling, and my therapist often brings elements of compassion-focused therapy into our sessions. They encourage me to think of my inner child when I'm struggling, and to treat myself like I'd treat that inner child. My other coping mechanism has always been comfort-eating. In my darkest hour after losing Khadija I was ordering McDonald's almost every day, sometimes twice a day. I was doing it to make myself feel better, and honestly in the moment it would feel better; but if I was to see my inner child, or any child, eating McDonald's twice a day, it would break my heart. That's what helped me to stop. Similarly, that's what helped me to stop hooking up, and I'm proud to say I haven't had a Big Mac in almost as long as I haven't had a big dick.

Thinking of my inner child in my everyday life has helped me to slowly realign myself, reassess what I want for myself and re-evaluate my core beliefs and values about myself and my relationships. I feel like I'm coming home to myself, growing into the person I'd dreamed I'd be when I was a child, making my inner child proud and protecting it at all costs.

I entered this lockdown spiralling out of control in a vicious cycle born of my romantic and platonic loneliness. And, ironically, it was being totally alone for a year that has meant I'm leaving lockdown free, feeling reset and re-energised, with a new consciousness, ready to defeat that loneliness. I'm gonna go get my life. Go get yours. Make your inner child proud.

Does Single Womanhood Bother Me?

CHLOE PIERRE

On the contrary, I have been raised by almost three generations of single women. They weren't always single, but the fact remains that they were at some point, especially when raising their children. At present I am a single woman, but I've also experienced the good, the beautiful, the bad and the ugly that comes with relationships.

Seeing single womanhood as normal has, at times, improved my self-confidence and has definitely propelled my decision to work hard for myself and to build the career, lifestyle and boundaries that I have and am constantly working on, and towards, today. I like to look at singledom now as being an intentional, determined and empowered act, all at the same time. Within the community in which I was raised, despite the high statistics of singledom and single-parent families, singledom is still often seen as a negative. However, despite this societal perspective, as a young woman, I have found this representation of family and the 'unit' successful, especially when raising modern young women – if, indeed, that is the goal. We should all be aware by now of the nuances in the terms 'modern', 'young' and 'women', as well as the contradictions and sometimes performative allyship, which often join arms with a subject like this. 'Yes to modern women, may we raise them, et cetera, but there's a limit' kind of thing. Coming from a succession of single-parent-only households, of course, I can tell you at first hand that raising a family single-handedly is extremely tough; it often comes without merit or thanks, and surviving it is only half the battle. But I have seen so many thrive on this journey, and I see it as a success, because it's not only battling the odds statistically, it's also battling the odds on a conscious societal level.

What have I learned about this journey – my journey of single womanhood?

I can't really answer that, as I'm still on this journey and it's forever changing, but I can tell you where I am right now. I'm looking deeper and further back to find the answers to help me, going forward. After getting back with my first-ever partner, becoming pregnant with him for the second time and experiencing physical, emotional and financial abuse, which I managed to escape – not without a number of bruises to both my confidence and my heart, but I somehow did this whilst being four months deep in said pregnancy – I'm still searching for answers. I say this, being one of the 'lucky people'. I made the choice to get out with immediate effect and have been able to hold my head high, even if only professionally or on social media. That, I have come to realise, is my superpower.

What I do know is how I feel, how I've felt and how I've been made to feel. Most importantly, I've learned how I want to feel going forward – regardless of being in a relationship or as a single woman – which is loved, cared for, respected and treated as both a woman and an equal.

My journey of reflection has had its stops and starts many times over the past few years, and I can directly contribute those experiences to helping me create my own movement and well-being business: thy.self. This reflection meant exploring my personal history, my DNA, my makeup, my childhood and my understanding of relationships from the very beginning. With therapy and a lot of secluded 'me time', I discovered that a consistent behavioural trait of mine is to keep integral parts of myself – my character and my being, for example – hidden or completely out of any public or intimate view. In short, for as long as I remember I have completely and practically felt less than, competed with, sometimes held down, and I think my 'nearest and dearest' – especially those who have continuously abused me, albeit creatively, over the years – have always felt very comfortable with that.

I often wondered, with the help of numerous and varied types of counsellors and therapy, if the reason for feeling like this, and this so-called reality, stems from childhood. But that's not what I remember from my childhood . . . or was it?

Growing up in a Black British Caribbean household and community, men were of course the dominant figures, but everyone knew it was the females who led (sometimes silently and sometimes not) and held our families together. There were no options other than to date and build homes with the opposite sex and, despite this being a 'partnership', the men I grew up around were broad-daylight kind of cheaters; some beat their partners, some abused their children, some even left the family unit altogether, or flittered across multiple homes and families without an ounce of remorse.

For the women in my community, yes, they were strong, but did they really know about self-love and self-respect? If they did, how was it demonstrated? I still can't answer that. So where was I expected to pick this up from?

What I didn't take into consideration was that my future romantic relationships weren't determined just by the theories I listed above. I want to point out that this is not a blame piece. This is my story and, with that said, I don't want said perpetrators to debate my reality with me. I like to think of this as a safe space to share my experiences, in the hopes that other women won't feel so confused, alone or, most simply – a term most relevant to today's culture – gaslit.

My own relationships with females in my family were to contribute to this. Our interactions were, and remain, key to my learning process. Where I'm from, we respect our elders, we share our experiences, sometimes we overshare, and sometimes by falling into these patterns we hinder each other and stunt the growth of younger generations coming of age with our own harrowing stories, albeit unintentionally.

I often questioned where physical and mental abuse in my adult and romantic relationships were coming from, and why they were so prevalent. I couldn't pick up on this anywhere else in my life. Of late, I have been analysing the relationships between myself and the women in my family. In particular, the relationship between my mother and me. I discovered that if my mother could break my spirit from a young age – diminishing how I talk, the way I look and dress, the friends I keep, my life choices, the business I run, questioning 'if I am' or 'act like' a Black woman – and compare me to others in my family who were placed on the pedestal, would it be absurd that someone I believed truly loved me couldn't do the same to me? Why is what he did to me different from what my mother did, and continues to do? Why is it OK for her, him or anyone else?

It's not.

Today I'm unafraid to report abusive behaviour. I am unafraid to stand up for myself, and how I may present myself to any other human being on this planet. I am free to exercise the boundaries that protect me, my mental well-being, my health and that of my unborn child.

Finding answers to the questions above has brought about highlights and lowlights, however I'm not prepared to let them hold me back. By putting this into writing, by reflecting and digging deeper, I'm freeing myself and my future; and in sharing this, I hope my story inspires actionable change for you.

So going back to the question: single womanhood doesn't bother me – whether I'm with child or not. I look forward to growing, healthily and with confidence. What bothers me is how normal abuse of all kinds is, and how hard it is to recognise this; the complex behavioural traits, the not speaking up and, most of all, the leaving it until it's 'too late'.

To the women reading this, you are my strength. You make being single worth it and, most importantly, it makes me proud to be single because I'm pushing back on what is not right.

If you have experienced or are experiencing abuse, know that you are not alone.* Whatever mistreatment you might have experienced

---

* Resources for reporting domestic violence can be found on page 35.

from a perpetrator, you didn't and don't deserve it, and it is not all you are worth.

I hope that, in reading this and taking it in, it's the first step for you to take back control of your life: how you think about yourself and how you are treated by people, going forward. If you feel unlovable or unloved at any stage of your journey, take time to learn how to love both the little bits and the bigger parts of you – even the ones that others may have tarnished. Regardless of what anyone says or how they behave towards you, you weren't put on this Earth to suffer. Choose to stop that, dead in its tracks, right now.

Recommended resources

- BAATN (therapy for people of colour) – www.baatn.org.uk/
- Clare's Law (the Domestic Violence Disclosure Scheme, to be used when you believe you are in a relationship with someone who perpetrates domestic violence; this disclosure is often given on a need-to-know basis of the alleged perpetrator's background of police reports and offences) – www.met.police.uk/advice/advice-and-information/daa/domestic-abuse/alpha2/request-information-under-clares-law/
- London Black Women's Project – www.lbwp.co.uk/
- Metropolitan Police (note to all women reading this: pressing charges and the laws around this are changing – find the courage to look into what options are available to you, including reporting incidents of domestic abuse after it has happened; there are no limits on when you can report a crime, and the Met can confirm this) – www.met.police.uk/
- National Domestic Abuse helpline – 0808 2000 247; www.nationaldahelpline.org.uk/
- Restraining Orders – www.gov.uk/injunction-domestic-violence/eligibility-non-molestation

- Sistah Space – www.instagram.com/sistahspace_/
- Skye Alexandra House – skyealexandrahouse.co.uk/
- Solace Women's Aid – www.solacewomensaid.org/
- Victim Support – www.victimsupport.org.uk/
- Women's Aid – www.womensaid.org.uk/
- Women's Refuge – www.refuge.org.uk/

Writing Your Own Story

FELICITY MORSE

My female inheritance has consisted of many stories. Lots of them with a distinctly romantic flavour, charting an onward course that stops abruptly at marriage and children. They are bad stories; more effective at putting me to sleep than helping me engage with life. But I didn't know any of this until I made friends with the pain of those storylines dissolving.

When I was seventeen I was at an all-girls boarding school. It was expensive, academic and renowned. Girls in my year had pop icons for godparents, came from a long line of intelligentsia, were born aristocrats or had families with billion-pound businesses. If you tore out a poster of someone famous from a magazine and stuck it on your bedroom wall, someone would either know them or be related to them. I was not one of these girls. My parents did well for themselves and we weren't poor by any means, but it still felt like a world I wasn't part of. I marvelled at it, whilst feeling like an outsider.

Ancestry aside, boarding school has this fantastic levelling quality. It doesn't really matter who your parents are – you're still seventeen years old, away from home, subjected to suffocating and contrary conditions. It was ridiculously socially controlled ('Don't go out after 5 p.m., it's dangerous; don't eat whilst walking, it's uncouth; don't dye your hair or wear make-up, it's tarty; don't fail tests, this is the best education in the country'), before descending into a kind of feral feminine *Lord of the Flies* when adult eyes were averted. It was intensely privileged, and also at times intensely miserable and lonely. There's no amount of accolades or gold-embossed Latin inscriptions that can help when you actually need a hug and someone to tell you it's all going to be all right.

The last term of school we had some former pupils come to talk to us about careers and what they did after leaving college. These stylish, intelligent women talked about setting up creative and successful businesses, and how they had evolved and adapted to flourish both financially and personally. The message underneath it all was that we could be empowered women in the workplace. We could choose, grow, explore. We could do things alone, be ourselves and make money. And at the end we were asked: does anyone have any questions?

A silence descended in the room. It had been a long and overwhelming afternoon of approaching adulthood. Then one girl put up her hand. She asked, 'So I'm wondering if, when you were here, you thought you'd never find a boyfriend and get married and have children?' Every one of us girls laughed, but the speakers and teachers were confused. It was completely unrelated to anything they had shared. But it was all we wanted to know. It felt like that girl had asked the question for all of us.

I'm sharing this story because it's stuck in my memory, and I always think stories that stick still have secrets to reveal. And also because, for me, it seems to encapsulate that it often doesn't matter how smart you are, how well resourced you are, how privileged your birth or bright-looking your future, the question of 'Who will I marry, to live out my happy-ever-after?' seems to take precedence.

Don't get me wrong: there's nothing wrong with that story, as long as you are sure it's yours. That you chose it, knowing you have other choices that are just as valid. There's nothing wrong with that story as long as it's not an exit plan. As long as you don't think that when you're living that story, all your problems will disappear. As long as you're not waiting for someone to rescue you from your own life.

Because I was. I didn't realise that some part of me had entwined my validity as a woman with being in a relationship, until I hit my late twenties and things felt off. It was strange to me, because I had a good job and I considered myself an empowered woman and a feminist. But there was a near-constant irritation that I was failing, and it seemed to focus around not having a partner. The reality wasn't matching up with what I thought would have happened automatically by this age. There was a low-level hum of time ticking anxiously – the future was arriving and it didn't look right.

I buried it. I told myself it didn't matter. I switched jobs into something I found more fulfilling. It kept me so busy I thought I had batted the story away, but instead I'd sent it underground. Yet the unconscious is a powerful force. As I approached thirty, these stories hit screech level, far away from my conscious 'girl about town' vibe. At the same time an incredibly charming, patient, intelligent and successful man entered my life. For the first time in seven years, I found myself in a relationship with someone who both wanted commitment and seemed to have the foundations to follow through on his intentions. I felt immensely relieved and happy that I had a partner, despite previously claiming I was totally fine without one, and that should have been a clue that something was happening here.

I had considerable professional success and had written a book at this point, but I would have felt like such a failure for not being in a relationship when I turned thirty – to not be able to point psychically to someone on this landmark birthday and say, 'Look, look, I'm not on my own, I have the future lined up, I'm doing it right; this high-status man wants me.' That storyline was so strong in my psyche that I needed to attract someone who would be willing to play it out with me. It was a compulsion and, like only the most dangerous compulsions, I was a hostage without recognising I was a prisoner.

And so it came to pass, almost inevitably, that this wonderful man, who impressed my parents, delighted my friends, ticked all the boxes, and who I had been coming to think of as my rock, was in fact a massive con man. Our romance was brought to a stuttering halt after he was charged with serious fraud. He was going to go on trial for conning investors based on a series of colossal lies. Criminal charges aside, the bulk of what he had told me about himself also wouldn't stand up in court.

Everything he had shared with me had either been entirely

untrue, someone else's truth, a projection, embellished so as to be unrecognisable from the truth or, in some cases, true now but achieved on a foundation of lies. Essentially there had been so much wanton cheating, manipulation, lying and storytelling as to make finding the truth an unrewarding project.

The heartbreak shook me awake. The extent of this man's amorality dwarfed anything I'd ever been in contact with before. And it wasn't altogether some cruel coincidence that we'd ended up together. I'd needed an actor to live out my romantic storyline, so no wonder I attracted someone incredibly good at acting. I was trying to live a life story that wasn't mine, and he was living a life that wasn't his, either. He acted out my story back to me (although mine wasn't conscious or criminally happening at someone else's expense, which is important for the character reference).

I felt deeply betrayed. I had lost not only the mirage-man in front of me, but all our rainbow-coloured romantic future. I lost trust, I lost confidence in myself, and for a while it felt like I lost hope in love. But what was really happening was that my storylines were shattering. And thank God. Because it gave a vital part of me the chance to write my own story.

So now I write my own life. And I make sure it's roomy; that I can expand with it and it can expand with me. I won't send a pre-chosen story out ahead of me, chopping myself up to fit it or to fit in. I write as I go and live the effervescence of each word. My life is more than a page-turner to race through, until the disappointing but predictable end. Instead I'll dance out the last syllables of every sentence, not knowing when the full stop will come, pausing breathless and alert when the beat stops, unexpectedly, for a moment. I'll allow myself to feel the dangerous, delicious, expansive freedom of not knowing what's next. I'll trust that I can co-create something beautiful with the universe, that will be perfect for just me, and it doesn't have to look like anything at all.

I'll afford myself the space to ask those soul-making questions, 'Who am I?' and 'Why am I here?', and wait with courage when the jaws of silence threaten to awaken my fears: that I have no meaningful identity, that not knowing who I am is in some way shameful, or that I can only be worthwhile as one piece of a romantic relationship, valid only if I produce children. I won't believe the voices that say my later years will be spent in self-recrimination and loneliness if I don't panic settle down. I will breathe them in, knowing that their appearance is initiatory, and will exhale the intensity in a long breath out, remembering how very human it is to feel like that, and to go on anyway and understand that as its own victory.

In male-dominated societies, women are often blocked from owning things. Denied even their own inheritance. But ownership is power. The right to own our inheritance and to choose what we pass on or don't pass on – that's a story that is not only important for me, but for who comes after me. And so I write my story for myself, but I write it for the woman who reads it, too.

For Every Single Woman Who's Ever Been Told She's the Problem - It's Not You

FRANCESCA SPECTER

For every single woman who's ever been told she's the problem, I see you, I hear you, I am you.

And I know that no matter how good the advice you give to your friends, no matter how clearly you can see their worth, their beauty, their kindness, their right to happiness – no matter how doggedly and sincerely you defend them at their lowest and most vulnerable – it's infinitely harder to be that same friend to yourself.

I know every disappointing date, every rejection, every 'Thing That Could Have Been a Thing' not working out after a couple of months – oh, I know the sting, the sensation of sliding back down a snake when you hoped you'd landed on a ladder.

I know the dating-app filters you adjust after every run of bad luck, thinking, 'Maybe I don't care, maybe I don't deserve this impossible Venn diagram of specifications, maybe attraction isn't all that important, maybe the joke made in poor taste was a defence mechanism' – in your lowest moments, whitewashing the reddest of flags to a more benevolent shade of pink.

I know the strange language you've learned, to navigate and normalise modern dating – ghosting, breadcrumbing, orbiting – the terms coined by lifestyle journalists and marketing gurus, cutesy vocabulary to justify the unjustifiable, the careless ways we drive each other crazy (because who knows the etiquette, really?).

I know the pain of a double blue tick, the evening vigil of an

'Online' status flickering on and off like a faulty light bulb, the slow erosion of hope over minutes, hours, days.

I know the God-awful sex, the kind you silently regret minutes in, politely putting their pride above your discomfort – the intimacy *sans* intimacy, eyes averted afterwards, if not during, no text back.

I know the insecurities, the slights, the 'Am I just being crazy?' thoughts that you discredit, burrowing them deep down in your heart, rationing out your pain to even your best friend.

I know, after a while, it's painful to even celebrate the good dates, to begin to fall in love, because of all the times you fell, badly, and it grazed your pride.

I know the mental arithmetic, the calculations: how long do I have to meet someone, to be married by thirty – have children by thirty-five – get divorced by forty-five? The ticking time-bomb as you go from playing the field to feeling frantic.

I know the trap of living dictated by other people's lives, rather than your own. Of using friends, siblings, your classmates, your ex as a yardstick. Of staying with the wrong partner, so you won't be alone on that group holiday. Of choosing to be the inwardly unhappy one, rather than the outwardly – and awkwardly – single one. Of compromising your one wild and precious life, to save face.

I know the distorted place of loneliness, the panic of an empty Saturday night, the false promises that maybe someone – anyone – will prove better company than your own thoughts. And then a stilted conversation, an awkward kiss, a £12 Uber is the price of valuing your solitude again, but it's too late: you've already traded in your evening; made the Faustian pact of choosing a stranger over yourself, because somehow, senselessly, it seemed easier.

I know that darker place, too – those Sunday nights when you lie awake past 1 a.m. turning over the faces of exes like Guess Who? cards in your mind, thinking, 'Was he really so bad, was I really so unhappy, could I have learned to love him despite myself?'

I know, of course, that it isn't all bad. I know the fresh perspective of a Monday morning, a reset if not redemption, the renewed focus and resilience.

And I know the inimitable joy of a jacket-potato dinner; of doing laundry-for-one; your clutter-free mind and kitchen surfaces; the silence you've come to love and are secretly scared you could never give up; the calm of closing the door behind you and knowing you're safe in your cocoon.

I know that you know there's more to life: the dream of travelling solo across New Zealand, the career change you're mustering up the courage for, the Glastonbury tickets, the marathon – all those things on your bucket list, the joys that could ignite your soul even though no one wrote a pop song about them (and perhaps even more so than love, because you're in control of your own happiness).

I know the joy of flirting with a stranger, feeling your most powerful, sexy self: confident and free, in a way no serious partner has ever made you feel, because tonight you have nothing to lose.

I know those nights when you fall into bed with your heart full, high on connection with your best friend, or your family, or a new group of strangers, and you wonder: just maybe, couldn't this be enough? Do I need to put myself through it all?

But, deep down, despite it all, you've retained that tiny piece of hope: as if burrowed away somewhere in your bedroom drawer, between your journal and your vibrator; stashed away in Tupperware alongside a long-forgotten, stale joint and a faulty Clipper; wrapped in tissue paper next to your late grandma's engagement ring and the memory box of you and the sixth-form boyfriend who broke things off when he left for Bristol.

The hope that you can finally invest, build something of substance, rather than a Jenga tower that comes tumbling down after date three. That you'll meet the person who wants to build it with you; to provide the scaffolding, the cement in the gaps you can't fill, and pave down a garden path towards your shared future.

The hope that, some day, someone worth the wait will swoop in and relieve you of being your own heroine, saving yourself, time and time again.

The hope that, decades from now, you'll be able to say: 'Dating is terrible, until it isn't.'

But that hope's wavering . . .

And you worry that maybe you're past repair – that you need to concede defeat, that maybe you should play safe, or not play at all.

And every time you say no to that second date with Mr Not Quite Right you feel that little bit less sure of yourself, less sure of your decision-making faculties, with echoes of relatives and friends in your head – she's too picky, she's been alone too long, she needs to learn to compromise.

Every time you poke your head outside the dating trenches, you pick yourself up and think, 'Maybe this time, maybe this one's different', but no sooner have you poked your head out than you get shot back down.

Every time you'd like to be a girl, standing in front of a boy, asking him to love her, but instead you're a nervous wreck navigating sporadic WhatsApp messages, inconsistent affections and a last-minute cancellation that you're trying not to read into, even though you know, deep down, it tells you everything you need to know.

Every time you think you've got it all worked out – you've worked on yourself, you've read all the books, you've taken up yoga, you've played the cool girl, you've chosen the good guy – but you get the same result.

And you get to the point when you think, 'Is it me? And would it be so strange if I were to, say, circulate a short, qualitative survey to the Ones Who Got Away (Because They Ran Away) – like a performance review, but for dating?' Unorthodox, perhaps, but surely so much more efficient than making the same mistakes again and again, going back out there, lamb to the slaughter, with that Thing that's so obviously wrong with you – the invisible spinach in your teeth – jeopardising your chances again and again.

For every woman who's ever been told she's the problem, I see you, I hear you, I am you. But I'm also not you – and, with the benefit of objectivity, I want to tell you this. And I want you to believe me.

It's not you – it's every rom-com plot that tells you to distrust your intuition, to ignore your own powers of judgement, because be honest, babe, how well has that worked out for you in the past?

It's not you, it's Generation Distraction – it's the undefined situationships, the DM slides, the myriad dating apps that build their business models around disconnection. You think you're gaming the system, filtering, swiping, typing until you find 'the one', but instead you're the one being gamified – along with your heart.

It's not you – it's the single supplement, the hotel rooms based on a couple sharing, M&S dine-in deals, two-for-one cinema tickets, the financial incentives to share your life with someone else.

It's not you – it's the well-meaning, open 'plus one' invitation that makes you think twice about calling things off before your best friend's wedding, because what could be worse than attending solo, minus one?

It's not you – it's the family members who ask if you've met someone, when you've virtually met everyone, and it makes you feel like you've failed, somehow, to find the needle in the haystack.

It's not you – it's the Tesco Food Love Stories campaign, where not one person eats alone (because the only story about you and your lasagne-for-one would be a tragedy, apparently).

It's not you – it's the generations of women who came before you, who were never shown a roadmap for being happily single and so try to 'save you' in the only way they know how to be saved.

It's not you – it's the clichés-for-two, 'Better Half', 'Significant Other', 'Life Partner', Soul Mate', which render you incomplete, by implication.

It's not you. It's falling back on the same, tattered archetypes – the Bridget Joneses, the Carrie Bradshaws – because twenty years on we have no better role models for being single.

It's not you. And maybe it's not them, either. The longer you date, the more you realise its arbitrariness; it's a question of fit, and timing, and sometimes geography. You can't peg your value on someone else's affections, simply because – both online and off – we're all merely flawed humans with our own insecurities, our own still-lingering flame for an ex, our (irrational but unignorable) gut instincts, our complicated childhoods.

It's not about you – or your worth, or your beauty, or your kindness, or your right to happiness.

It's just the way it is.

And the only tragedy is the system that makes you think you are the problem, that you alone are responsible for your failure to find love. That being single is, in itself, a failure.

Besides, in love, no one really wins. But no one really loses, either. Because love is vulnerability; love is long; love is messy, complicated and thrilling; it's accepting that you have to make a leap of faith before you can really stand to gain anything. Finding love is a beginning, not a happy ending. It's not a blanket solution; it's a set of novel problems. It's as much about loving as being loved. It's about making it work. It's about—

But what the hell do you know, anyway? Who are you to speak about relationships, when yours have always ended? Not that it matters, right now. Because this isn't about shared love. This is about you, navigating through it all as a single person – an individual holding the weight of your hope. And that weight can be a lot to carry alone. It can crush you.

And yet you need to keep that fire alive within you, that hope against hope that maybe, some day, all the bullshit will be rendered worthwhile. Not in an instant, but perhaps in that moment that sets all the other moments into motion, a domino effect that makes you look back one day – in thirty years, perhaps – and say: If only I'd known where all of this was leading to.

Because maybe, on some level, it *is* you. And do you really want to know what's wrong with you? It's that, secretly, you're too romantic for your own good. That you've always been that way. That you're no hardened sceptic; you're an idealist – deprived of your coupled-up friends' vantage point, the rows about left-up toilet seats. That yours is the greatest love story of them all, because it hasn't happened yet – because you've spent so many years refining it in your head.

That your high standards were never really about height or hairlines, but about a Big Love – a love proportionate to all those nights you waited in for the call that never came; all those break-up

For Every Single Woman Who's Ever Been Told She's the Problem

texts; all that swiping; all those weddings attended Minus One; all those knock-backs; all that intimacy-less intimacy; all that playing it cool – playing with fire – owning your desire; all those fucking Ubers to SE15.

That somewhere along the way you lost sight of yourself, in your quest for 'the one'. That you've devalued your affections through frittering them away on people who never even asked for them, giving away your diamonds for free, handing them out on the street, forgetting that no one can value you more than you value yourself, right this moment.

That your value is defined not by their love – yes, even when you meet your person – but by the love you invest in yourself daily. And right now, you need that love more than ever.

That you've been investing in the wrong candidate, because the sole person deserving of this amount of loving and dreaming and analysing was only ever yourself: the one lifelong relationship you'll ever have.

The ironic part is, you probably won't be single for ever. And I say that not as a consolation, but as a warning.

Love is a losing game – but that loss isn't about any specific person. It's not about losing face. It's about losing faith: your capacity to love with your whole heart, generously, intuitively, freely.

And that's not all you risk losing – far from it.

It's losing your capacity to be curious; to listen; to be (pleasantly) surprised; to be seduced; to take things slowly, to savour them.

It's losing those weeks, months, years, to heartbreak, lost to someone whose name you'll barely remember one day, whose once-beloved face you'll cross the street to avoid.

It's losing all that time spent in a waiting room, imagining your life will begin the moment you meet this mysterious person, your Prince Charming to share a Chinese takeaway – then realising, too late, that the grass isn't greener; that you were sold a con that stopped you from living for years, decades.

It's losing your potential to grow, after so much time spent folding yourself up, moulding yourself to fit what you think they might want.

It's losing sight of your goals, your passions, your capacity for connection – your bright future – because no one ever told you there was another way to be single, other than reluctantly, apologetically, uncomfortably.

It's losing on leading a Big Life, so fixated are you on finding the Big Love to begin it with.

For every single woman who's ever been told she's the problem, I see you, I hear you, I am you. One day, things will change. You'll meet Someone. And maybe they won't live up to the vision in your head, but you'll take that person in your arms, instead, because they're real, and that's better anyway. But right now, my darling, choose yourself.

Eat, Pray, Run

JESSICA MORGAN

Jake* was my longest and most serious relationship. We had been together for four years. Four long, wonderful years until, one day, he broke up with me in a Starbucks around the corner from my office in Bank. 'I don't love you any more,' he told me over a Pumpkin Spice Latte. I was shocked, confused and started laughing because I thought it was a joke. It must have been. We had spent four years – four magical years – in love. At least in my head. Unfortunately, I was wrong. He really did mean it and, despite pleading with him in the middle of my favourite coffee shop, he never came round. I accepted it, finished my coffee and headed home.

A few days later he texted me. 'We still have those tickets to Winterville on Saturday, shall we go?' It seemed an odd request, as I had just been dumped. But I thought he had changed his mind and so I agreed, giddily. Except that he didn't change his mind, and that day we awkwardly walked around what was supposed to be a romantic wintery festival among other couples who looked far happier than we did. We headed for the Backyard Cinema, where we had tickets to see *Mary Poppins*, a childhood favourite of both of us. We had pre-booked, with our entry tickets, a bottle of champagne and treats. When we were escorted to our seats – a giant beanbag with cushions and blankets – I thought this would be where Jake would make a U-turn on his cruel dumping and tell me how much of a mistake he had made. He didn't, and every time I tried to reach his hand to hold, he pulled away.

---

* A pseudonym.

When the film ended, we stood opposite each other in Victoria Park in silence. 'So are we not getting back together,' I asked sheepishly.

'No,' he responded.

'So what was the point in us coming here? Wasn't this supposed to be romantic?'

'Well, it was better than wasting the tickets,' he responded coldly. I realised this was the end, but what a way to do it. I felt tears fall down my face and I got hot and flustered, embarrassed as people passed us by.

'OK, well, I'm going home,' I said and walked to Mile End station, a few yards from where we lived together for half our relationship. It was a bitter end, and one I didn't get over for the next six months.

When I got home I cried on my kitchen floor and felt an emptiness I had never felt before. Was this heartbreak? I went to text Jake, to say thank you for an enjoyable day – the message remained undelivered and unread. We never saw each other again.

I had to learn to be alone after my break-up, which was incredibly hard when you're used to having someone around every day. Every day I woke up with anger at the sudden change in my lifestyle, my schedule and my social life, but it was a rude awakening. I realised that I had put so much of myself into this relationship that I had lost a part of myself: my independence and my mind. I fell into a deep depression – a part of me that had been lingering for some time and was left untreated. It was my secret, and one I hadn't spoken about publicly before, but something inside me wanted to set myself free.

Before Jake and I broke up, I had run the Berlin marathon. A lot of our relationship was around running, and he was the one who got me into long-distance running. But one evening, as I sat in tears on my bed thinking about what I could do for myself, I googled 'adventure marathons' and searched frantically for somewhere, far away, that I could travel to alone. I had admired Elizabeth Gilbert's *Eat, Pray, Love* and her journey to Italy and Bali to find herself, and I saw a lot of myself in her. I was desperate to get away, to immerse myself in a completely different culture where I could be out of my comfort zone, to recalibrate.

So in May 2016 I jetted off to China. I was about to run the Great Wall of China marathon. I travelled alone, having not learned any Mandarin (although I had bought a Lonely Planet guidebook, which had phrases, in the English and not the Chinese alphabet, that proved utterly useless), and landed in Beijing with not the faintest clue what I had got myself into. It was an adventure, a spontaneous adventure, that I had set myself on and I was nervous and excited in equal measure.

Once I landed, I was introduced to the runners who would be joining me along the way. Rasmus, a tall, blond man from Sweden, who looked very serious. He told me in his thick Scandinavian accent that he had run the Boston marathon the year before I did, and we bonded in the taxi on the way to our hotel – over our love of the many kisses we received from the Wellesley College students along the route, and the famous Boylston Street finish line – all while clinging on for dear life as our driver zigzagged his way through the unmarked streets of Beijing.

I didn't know anyone else running the marathon, so I was forced to make new friends and socialise, something that I had lost during my depression, and I had developed social anxiety from having my relationship ripped from underneath me. I had to rebuild myself again to become Jessica before my relationship. And it was difficult, but I was determined. I met Robert, a well-built, middle-aged Black man from America, who wore a black tank top that read 'Black Men Run Too' and whose personality lit up every room he walked into. Then Val, an outspoken South African woman, who had run more than fifty marathons and ultra-marathons. And Roel, a gay Filipino man who made me laugh every minute of the day. And Amy, my roommate, who kept me up all night, giggling as we traded skincare tips. My new friends, from all over the world, taught me something important. They had all travelled to China alone for a reason: Robert had just gone through a painful divorce, Val wanted a new challenge, Roel had lost both his parents, and Amy wanted to prove to herself that she could run a marathon. It made me feel seen.

One day we went to the Forbidden Palace. Our tour guide, Lily, carried with her a flag for us to look out for, so we didn't get lost. In her broken English she said, 'Don't lose yourselves!', which made me laugh, because I knew what she meant, but it had a far greater meaning. 'Don't lose yourself' was poignant to me and has stayed with me ever since. While the whole purpose of me travelling to China was to run a marathon on the Great Wall, I was also there to find myself again.

Then, on 14 May 2016, I took this message with me along for the ride. As my legs ran ahead of me, taking each steep step in my stride, I took a deep breath once I reached the top. 'I'm on one of the Seven Wonders of the World, I feel alive,' I thought, and I burst into tears. After experiencing so much pain from my break-up, being on top of the Great Wall made me realise that if I could complete a marathon here, nothing else could step in my way.

When I got home from China I had a new lease of life and a fresh perspective on how I perceived myself as a single young woman living in London. I no longer felt the desperate need for one central relationship and I continued to work on myself. I joined running clubs, I made new friends and I challenged myself with new opportunities. They always say that if you can't love yourself, you can't afford to love anyone else, and it's true. I was single for six years since Jake and I broke up, and I had never felt more confident by myself.

But, at the height of the coronavirus pandemic, I found love with a man who I am excited to share my life with. I have appreciated the time I have spent by myself, but I opened my heart to someone who supports and inspires me every single day to be better. As a young woman, there's always pressure on us to find someone special, especially if you're teetering towards your thirties. But if love hadn't crept into my life the way it did, I still would have been happy. Single or in a relationship, I understand the true joy of being alone and enjoying alone-time, without panicking that there isn't anyone by my side. I have appreciated the true value of solitude, alone-ment (as my dear friend Francesca Specter says), as well as the ability to choose who I want around me.

I have found joy, today, tomorrow and forever.

Singlehood Unlimited: Solo Living in South India

KETAKI CHOWKHANI*

Ode to my Community
The great are strongest when they stand alone.
A God-given might of being is their force,
A ray from self's solitude of light the guide;
The soul that can live alone with itself meets God . . .

When I was little, my teachers inspired me. One of them came to class with a black dog named Snow White in tow; another lived alone in a large, beautifully decorated home; and another worked at a farm on the weekends. All of them, except for a few, were single and never married. Their homes, their lives, their affection for animals, their love for the subjects they taught, their passion for art and beauty and their warmth towards their students marked my childhood. Growing up in a not-so-perfect home with varying levels of approval, I felt that my school was my source of comfort. I knew my teachers accepted me, just the way I was – gawky, weird, solitary and passionate about writing, art, cinema, nature and dogs. I spent a large portion of my co-curricular time learning art, and all my art teachers were single, and mostly women. They took us to all kinds of places to draw *en plein air*, their passion for the subject infectious.

Most of these teachers were part of a spiritual community in

---

* I would like to thank Ranjana Saha for discussions and support in writing this essay.

South India where I grew up. It was not a place for following social norms. The two radical founders of the community, Aurobindo Ghose and Mirra Alfassa, left their respective spouses at the beginning of the twentieth century to form a sanctuary for intense spiritual seeking. They actively discouraged marriage. No permanent member of the community was supposed to get married. In their correspondence with disciples, they made it clear that marriage 'is a terrible bondage', a social custom that holds no significance, a childish, amusing idea. Since the community was for spiritual seekers, they held that marital life and spiritual life lay in opposite directions and could only be a stage in human evolution. They also noted that for those who held spiritual values, the breakdown and disappearance of the family system were important, and that a diversity of ways of living and child-rearing was necessary for human progress.

Most permanent community members follow these ideals and, unlike some of us children who grew up with families and married parents, they live in what we today call co-housing. Each member is allotted a room of their own, while dining, cultural activities, work, laundry and medical care are communal. They are not residentially alone, but live in intentional communities. The community takes care of all their material needs, which frees them up for community work and spiritual growth. This is a scaled-down version of a welfare state, which provides a safety net allowing larger numbers of people to go solo. To grow up in this community was, for me, to be surrounded by thousands of single, never-married people, who lived alone. Scholars have pointed to the dearth of single role models for a growing child, and here I was, able to draw on a rich legacy of single life.

Not only were my teachers single, but they also taught me integral education. Today I realise the invaluable role that integral education plays in happy singlehood. Integral education, developed around the 1940s by Mirra Alfassa and Aurobindo Ghose, encourages a holistic, all-round development of the human being. It places no importance on material success, but is driven by perfection and transformation of the human being. A few decades later, in the 1970s, post-materialism arose. With economic stability, people began to value freedom, self-expression, creativity and self-actualisation. Research has shown that singles who hold post-materialist values are more likely to be happier and fulfilled in their lives. Post-materialist values are in consonance with integral education; both reject utilitarianism and value self-actualisation and the spirit of newness and discovery. My initiation in integral education automatically included a generous dose of post-materialism, which today helps me lead a better and happier single life. I owe my happy singlehood today to the founders of my community and to their vision of life and integral education.

> **Singing Singlehood: Living the Best Life**
> I row my own canoe
> Do not believe in fairy tales
> Which end in a story of two.
> Whom will you belong to?
> Why, no one, I say
> I belong to sky and trees
> And every living being.
> Who will be by your side
> When the wind draws near?
> No one, and everyone.
> In this tiny world of twos
> I stand alone and together
> I row my own canoe.

Research has pointed to the various benefits of solitude, especially those related to creative pursuits. It has also shown that single people are socially seen to have empty time and lives, since they lack a partner and family. But my life and time couldn't be fuller. Making music wasn't the only creative pursuit that filled my spare time. I also experienced the renewed pleasure of photography, putting to use a much-neglected camera. I took it with me during my numerous solo birding walks and discovered anew the joys of nature, from its vast expanses to its minute details. I discovered the art of solo travel and adventure by taking short day-trips or going sea-swimming or kayaking alone, much to the consternation of those around me. Occupying a table for one at a restaurant or going to the theatre alone wasn't new for me, but the delights were many. The solitude of living alone and freedom over my own time gave me ample space to explore hitherto-unknown sides of myself.

Theorising and Teaching Singlehood
The Sole in its solitude yearned towards the All
And the Many turned to look back at the One.

These lines aptly sum up the singlehood standpoint that I have been developing since 2019; they synthesise the scholarship on singlehood and my personal experiences narrated so far. I contend that a singlehood standpoint, which emerges out of single people's lives, is a way we relate to other human beings, to non-humans and to ourselves. I claim that if we use this standpoint we will be more likely to relate to the world of other human beings through communities, and instead of focusing on one central relationship – like a marriage – we will have emotionships, and will be able to forge connections beyond our families. Using this standpoint will also help us relate to non-humans by using creativity, post-materialism and integral education. Lastly, a singlehood standpoint will help us to connect better with ourselves through solitude. It is an orientation that anybody can adopt; I maintain that it will help create a fundamentally different self and society.

It has taken me years to develop and nurture this standpoint, and teaching singlehood has played a major role in it. In January 2020 I was fortunate enough to be able to design and teach India's first ever Singles Studies course at postgraduate level. Singles Studies aims to address the neglected category of the single person across disciplines. It argues for the inclusion of a single person's fresh perspective on various issues, like family, gender, time, ageing, the city, law, geography and medicine. If a singles perspective is to be integrated in research, it cannot merely be additive. It has to transform the way we approach research. The course challenged students' preconceived notions regarding romance and coupledom, and urged them to look at the world through a single person's lens. The teaching and discussions in class informed my research and life, urging me to be:

> One with the Transcendent, calm, universal,
> Single and free, yet innumerably living,
> All in thyself, and thyself in all dwelling,
> Act in the world with thy being beyond it.

The Decade Challenge

LUCIE BROWNLEE

It was my first foray into online dating; my first-ever date since my beloved husband Mark had died suddenly, aged just thirty-seven, in February 2012. How could I have known, then, that you should never commit to more than a quick coffee with any potential beau because of that photo on their profile of them looking buff on the beach in Alcúdia? It is almost certainly pinched from their much better-looking mate Dave's Instagram. Yet here I was, having agreed to a whole night out with the first guy who asked, and who, inevitably, looked nothing like his picture and had a voice like Joe Pasquale's. As I drove home (early, on some spurious pretext) I forgave myself my naïve folly through a blurry screen of tears.

It wasn't meant to be like this, of course. I wasn't supposed to be back in the dating game aged thirty-seven. I was meant to be wrung out, with two kids, a dog and a mortgage; and a husband to complain about to my other married friends. As it stood, I had a tiny daughter, no dog, no mortgage and no husband, and a dating profile that listlessly informed future suitors that I liked Wagamama noodle bowls and red wine.

At first I'd stridently proclaimed that I would never date another man. It had taken me long enough to find Mark; and besides, it would be disloyal to his memory. I held dear to this stance for about ten months, and then the 'for everness' of the situation began to sink in (along with the thought of going through life without ever having another shag). A friend tactfully told me to stop being Widow Twanky and pointed me in the direction of Match and my fateful date with old Joe.

There came a compulsion to be promiscuous. I bought out the

whole Primark lingerie department and pursued anything with a penis. I had a raucous fling with a plumber who came to fix a leaky tap. I went on a handful of drunken dates with a guy ten years my junior. This all made me feel desired, proved that I still had it, that my widowed status did not mean condemnation to a life of Queen Victoria after Albert. Married friends looked on with the kind of expression one might reserve for a particularly brutal death scene on Attenborough's *Planet Earth*, but I convinced myself that they were jealous, shackled as they were to the boring old marital bed.

What they didn't see, though, were the endless lonely nights in between all the screwing. The nights when I'd sob in great ugly jags for Mark, shout pleas into an empty room for him just to come back; when I'd have given anything to feel his warmth beside me in the boring old marital bed. They didn't witness the times my daughter, then four or five, had held me in her small embrace and told me, 'Don't worry, Mummy, everything is going to be OK.' Or the darkest moments, in which the void left by the love of my life felt too huge to bear.

I started my first 'serious' relationship about eighteen months in. He was a good guy, but it was all too soon for such leaps of emotional faith. It felt as if I missed Mark more when I was in a committed relationship, as opposed to the random cock-hopping that went before it. We hobbled along together for almost two years, Good Guy and I – he trying his best to accommodate my frequent and messy bouts of grief, and I trying my best to be the devoted partner he craved, all the while feeling guilty for still being hopelessly in love with a dead man. Eventually we agreed to set each other free. (He is now married with a child of his own – which he deserves and is all he ever wanted.)

I persisted with the online dating, expanding my repertoire to a couple of other sites. It never sat comfortably with me, the online stuff, mainly because it all felt so transactional and failed to acknowledge my need for subconscious attraction, which can't be gauged through scrutiny of a few photographs. I signed up to one site and immediately rescinded my membership after being launched, screaming, into a melee of buff imposters-on-beaches and men who *didn't want no drama.* My profile picture was still an egg, yet I received an avalanche of messages telling me I was hot. So much for the discerning gentleman.

Then came The Widower. Reader, I was so in love. Not only did we have a tragic shared experience of premature spousal loss, but we seemed to click with each other on that subconscious level I mentioned earlier. Together with our collective offspring, we embarked on a love affair of which I only could have dreamed. Some people never get one chance at true love, and here was I, warming my cockles at the fireplace of my second! For two years we revelled in the possibility that we were the other's next chapter, until one cold January afternoon it all went up in smoke. He needed time with his kids, he said, and had no emotional capacity for me and mine. I told him I would wait. And I did – but it turned out he'd already moved on with someone else.

I had never really been alone before. There had always been someone to fill the gap, in one way or another. After The Widower, my faith in love and men was totally shattered. I found myself grieving once again, and I knew how much time and energy it would take to rebuild. I made a decision not to allow in anyone close enough to break my heart again.

As I write, it's been a decade since Mark died. Four years since the relationship with The Widower ended and here I am, still unattached. However, in that time I have found myself again; a new version, who is stronger, bolder and more creatively charged than ever. I have invested my energy in precious friendships, old and new. Most of all, I have relished watching my daughter grow and change, and I continue to nurture a profound and beautiful relationship with her. She looks so much like her dad and has mannerisms of his, which can only be innate. Now thirteen years old, she is my gift from him, my soulmate – the love of my life.

There will always be a part of me that is missing, a part that died with Mark. For too long I tried to patch over the missing part, believing it could somehow be repaired or replaced. With time – a long time – I have accepted that it can't, and I have learned to live without it. I have tentatively reopened my heart to the prospect of meeting someone new, but I'm in no rush. If it happens, I will feel fortunate and grateful – and so should he. If it doesn't, I will still feel fortunate and grateful: for my daughter, for my family and friends, and for having had the privilege of once being loved by Mark.

Though this road has been tortuous, with many potholes along the way, I am finally at peace.

Sunday

MADELEINE SPENCER

I was always very bad at Sundays; I considered that empty seventh day of the week to be my enemy. It unwrapped me of the busy schedule belonging first to school, then to university, then to work, leaving me emotionally naked without distractions, stranded solo.

The first time I realised that being without somewhere to be, or someone to see on Sunday, was challenging was at the age of six. My parents were both still asleep, my older siblings engaged in whatever they were into at the time (it was the eighties, so I like to imagine it was Cabbage Patch Dolls and a Rubik's Cube, them wearing Hypercolor and listening to New Kids on the Block). I'd just finished my Corn Flakes when the melancholy that has characterised my Sundays since descended and, not quite knowing what it was or how to escape it, I picked up a Roald Dahl book and let the story swallow me whole.

And so it continued, Sundays offering up a smorgasbord of sadness and flatness and an unshakeable sense of time ticking by, with me suspended in what felt like a spider's web of complicated emotions, unable to make anything of the day, ever more unhappy and entangled every time I fought it. Escapism was my relief: into a book, into a film, into someone else's company. It worked, for the most part, filling the time, if not completely squashing the blues.

Sunday presented itself in different forms over the years. As a child there were birthday parties with cakes suffocated under lashings of icing; Sunday roasts swimming in gravy; afternoons spent doing homework long overdue; the distant, dissonant, tinny cry of an ice-cream van that we could never quite locate, despite it always sounding nearby; the shops I wanted to buy sweets from being shut; endless, endless, endless mulchy leaves on endless, endless, endless walks through forests as a fog of gloom clustered around my small shoulders.

Later, it would look different but feel the same. Sunday became the day after Saturday – Saturday being *the* night, the apex of all weekday dreams. Would *that* song play at the party? Would *that* boy kiss me? Would *that* outfit make me feel like a cross between J Lo and Kylie Minogue? (Spoiler: it never did, but I continued to try every single Saturday throughout my late teens, irrespective of the vast gap between sumptuous hope and soggy reality.) Sunday was bereft of anticipation, the fantasies evaporated and all that remained was discussing what had happened the night before, over toast and milkshakes with friends while waiting for Monday, when the wheels would once again start turning.

But Sundays mutated when I embarked on my first big relationship. Together, he and I faced it. Was it a better day for being someone's girlfriend? Arguably no, not in essence, not really – but having a partner in my misery lessened the intensity of it, and together we did those things characteristic to the day, stuffing the nothingness with activities that must have been inspired by a romcom, so cringingly obvious were they. We snuggled under blankets when it was rainy, binging on films, breaking for sex or food, reading aloud the amusing snippets from the papers. When sunny, we'd go for those endless, endless, endless walks that were a staple of my childhood, occasionally slipping into a museum if we were feeling up to playing the role of being terribly cultured. We would even sometimes call each other 'babe', which I now realise absolutely must have been borrowed from a film, because in my unadulterated state I wouldn't ever do such a thing.

In any case – babe or not, sleepy sex to a soundtrack of Bic Runga or not – it came to an end after arguments started to puncture holes in our idyll. We broke up on a blazing hot Sunday, during the sort of heatwave that's rare enough in London to be newsworthy. It was also flying-ant day, the floor strewn with them – me gingerly padding between their bodies while wearing some exquisite but extortionate sandals that had been the cause of an argument;

he deemed them impractical for a forest walk; I decided that he was categorically wrong and also cruel to try to deny me the pleasure I was so clearly deriving from wearing them.

I felt very strongly about it – so strongly that, following crossed words, I decided to leave and this time for good. Off me and my sandals went to the Tube station, each step taking me further away from the buoy I'd clung to, returning me to the dark prospect of Sundays alone again.

Two things happened after that. First, Sundays got worse. Quite a lot worse. All the old feelings were back, and the contrast between them plus or minus an ally was considerable. I felt flatter, emptier, sadder. I yearned for someone to take it all away, to provide a wall between me and that wretched day. I equated feeling painfully single with Sundays, a day when it felt requisite to have a partner – especially in my mid-twenties, when group dinner parties and BBQs were very much a Saturday fixture, and Sundays were characterised by that combination of relaxing and preparing for the week ahead, both activities that friends were never invited to partake in.

There was a dinner party one weekend that compounded my misery. Everyone was tipsy, dancing ensued, six people who'd arrived alone departed as three couples after exchanging very indiscreet kisses to whoops of encouragement, and everyone left knowing they'd wake with sore heads. I was the only attendee who wasn't walking *à deux* the next day or indulging in some shagging – I was sipping my tea, steeped in Sundayness, and I was sure that escaping singledom by rekindling things with my ex was to be my fate.

The other thing that happened changed that. The ex started to send emails. The first was a tentative hello. I didn't reply. The next was to tell me he was now living with a new girlfriend and was terrifically happy. I was hurt, but didn't reply. Then came the email he'd clearly wanted to send from the off: an invitation to rendezvous, despite him professing to be happy in his new relationship. I quite genuinely considered replying. But then my strength and spirit rose to the surface and I realised that I had allowed a man

I knew to be a rather bad egg remain in my life because I was afraid. And that realisation made me so much more afraid of a life of dependency, a life of compromise, that I decided I really had to face my thing about Sundays head-on.

Sundays were shit. This I unequivocally believed to be true. But maybe I could take on a rubbish day once a week alone? Of course I could. Of course it was fine. Of course I felt stronger, more able to handle whatever or whoever life would throw my way, for having weathered the bleakness of sitting alone in my flat for the entire five January Sundays that hit, right after my resolution.

It turned out that quite a few Sundays would pass before I found someone I wanted to be with, who wanted to be with me. I waited patiently, each week throwing myself into my work and friendships, then letting it wash its mucky stew of emotions over me. I watched it roll in, and I watched it roll away again, each time affecting me less.

When I met someone, I wanted to be with them not because they take away the gloom on one day, but because they could add something to my life as a whole every day. It made all the difference, to me and to the relationship, not fearing Sundays any more.

Unapologetically Unattached

MEGAN BARTON-HANSON

I'm twenty-seven and have been single for three years.

You could say I am getting fussier with age. My standards are so much higher now. When I was younger I would go for the guy with the washboard abs, flashy sports car and spray-on jeans, whose favourite topic of conversation was how he had the most hectic week batting back the women and stacking cash he made on stocks.

Now, I am open to dating men and women. These days it's not purely based on physical attraction. See, the type I mentioned above is great for casual sex, but I would say the two people I have loved the deepest, I didn't even fancy initially – it was their energy I fell in love with.

There is a rather archaic view within society that women must settle down as they approach the age of thirty. I'm – hand on heart – the happiest I've ever been in the last couple of years, being single. But there was a younger version of me that saw being single as absolute hell. Who would I travel with? Who would I go for dinners with? How would I feel when everyone was posting pictures of their other halves at their birthdays, at Christmas or on Valentine's Day?

I feel embarrassed (and sad) that I used to have that mentality. I used to think, 'I'm successful, financially stable, and made my whole career from men wanting to see me naked or date me. I don't deserve to be single!' But I had it all wrong. Unfortunately for me, whilst I'm usually so stubborn and unapologetic in other areas of my life, I was buying into the false concept that being single is a result of you being unsuccessful. The media, films and

TV shows – the perfect couple, the perfect family and the perfect life, all with a warm and fuzzy happy ending. That was seen as the goal, and anything that looked different was not approved by society.

After a bad break-up I forced myself to go away alone. Just Spain, and other places in Europe at first. Checking into a hotel for the first time and being asked why you are alone can be awkward – most definitely made worse by the fact that I am naturally introverted. And going for a meal for the first time alone isn't comfortable at all. Especially when I'm told by waiters that I'm too pretty to be single and eating alone, and families and couples tell me, 'Come and sit with us! Don't be on your own!' So pity was prevalent; couple that with fears when walking back to the hotel, tipsy after the dinner, and it was a bit of a nerve-racking experience, to say the least. However, I truly believe, as with anything in life, that unless you feel fear and do it anyway, you won't grow.

After that first solo trip, I flew to LA and Miami and met amazing people, single and alone. I had lots of friends who would have joined me, but I felt like it was important for me to grow and realise that being single will not stop me doing what I want.

I reckon that is why there has been this sense of failure or shame instilled in us from a young age – thinking that being thirty and single is a negative. In reality, by your late twenties you actually start caring less what others think, and start doing *you*. Girls in their late twenties are just coming into their own and feeling more secure. We've already done it all: players and one-night stands; the rich guy (who we envision will send our kids to boarding school but really has a total lack of personality, made palatable due to the prospect of being financially stable); the broke artist, who is so deep and speaks painfully slowly; the musician (who thinks he is cooler than you . . .). I realised that the constant need for a partner can be so boring and unnecessary – being content with being alone is so important.

Unfortunately for us, society has other ideas. Relatives deem it appropriate to ask at every family gathering if you're still single; journalists can seem genuinely concerned that I'm still alone – and have even gone so far as to ask me how I would conceive and who would carry our kids, since I've been publicly dating women. The audacity.

The last relationship I had was probably the hardest break-up I've ever dealt with, since I was in the public eye. It really is a whole new world. With the guy I met on *Love Island* there was an incredible amount of pressure to make the relationship work. Again, feelings of failure crept in, when I had to face the hard truth that the relationship was breaking down. I think due to the fact that we met on a reality show, many people had doubted the legitimacy of the break-up from the get-go anyway, and that added to the pressure immensely. My feelings were genuine, and having to prove that repeatedly in interviews and on social media was so draining. I didn't know any other way, either, as I experienced fame almost overnight.

I must say it didn't help being painted as the man-eater/femme-fatale character on the show. I felt like everyone would have been happy to see the relationship fail. I feel like people forget that we are human and, for me, my feelings were real.

When my partner at the time booked another show and I was invited to watch, the narrative from *Love Island* continued. I was portrayed as an insanely jealous villain – I was even caught not smiling for two seconds, and that made headlines. I'd had enough. I had to draw the line. This was my life – not a pantomime. I realised that I had to start looking after myself. My mental health was way too precious to continue struggling in a relationship just because I was proud and wanted to prove the public wrong.

Intrusive questions from journalists were a shock and can still catch me off-guard. There is almost a sense of entitlement, since I found fame on a reality show. Journalists think they can ask about every aspect of my personal life. I'm a sex-positive, honest and straightforward person, but I'm starting to feel like there should be things kept private in every relationship to make it special. That was probably the hardest thing about a public break-up. There is ridiculously more pressure on women than on men to maintain the relationships. I feel like men don't get judged, based on their dating status. They can be single into their late thirties and forties and it is never seen as an issue. We have seen prime examples of this within TV shows over the years – serial male daters who are seen as heart-throbs, whilst women who are single at thirty are seen as victims and in a frantic rush to freeze their eggs. Is anyone else incredibly bored of this narrative? This portrayal of women being deemed less, for being without a man, is so outdated and offensive.

Lockdown has really taught me that being alone can be so enjoyable. For starters, I don't have to please anyone else. I've put all the energy I used to put into looking for someone, or forcing a dead relationship, into myself. I have learned so much about who I am, what I enjoy and what I seek in life. I have reached a point where I've learned to love who I am – flaws and all. Whilst I am open to dating, if the right person comes along, I am by no means panicking because of my age.

I am grateful that the younger me took the time to get to really know myself, address previous traumas and heal from them. I have started focusing on working hard, connecting with friends and family more closely and gaining true life experiences. I believe this will also make any future relationship a healthier and better experience. I know now that I will never again stay in a situation where I am unhappy, and that is a lesson I am so glad I have learned. Life really is too short.

Dismantling the Dreamhouse

MIA LEVITIN

I was never one to stage weddings in the Barbie Dreamhouse, preferring to play with my *Star Wars* figures and GI Joes. Unlike action figures, which – as their name implies – are designed to do stuff, there wasn't much to act out with Barbie, apart from wardrobe changes and playing house. (Even her make-out sessions with Ken and Stacie were thwarted by the dolls' drawn-on drawers.) 'I have a date tonight!' said an early model of Talking Barbie when you pulled her string. 'Which new dress shall I wear?'

Since I'd never fantasised about a wedding, it surprised everyone when I was the first of my friends to get engaged, in my early twenties. First in, first out: I was the first to divorce, too. When my marriage ended after twelve years, I figured I had chosen the wrong person, but didn't question for a second the notion that having a partner was necessary for long-term fulfilment. I may have escaped Barbie's influence, but the culture at large persisted with a double standard for singletons. Unmarried men were bachelors – a word that continues to connote cool. While Barbie frets over frocks, Talking Ken plots his seduction: 'Let's go listen to Barbie's records,' he spouts suggestively. An unmarried woman, by contrast, is a spinster. If I didn't act fast, I was destined to end up with only cats for company.

Hell-bent on hunting down Mr Right 2.0, I embarked on dating armed with an Excel spreadsheet and love coach-to-the-stars. If you had told me when I divorced that I would still be single after more than a hundred first dates, I would never have believed you. But truth be told, I'm grateful for the time alone. Women are conditioned from childhood to put their faith in romantic love. As it turns out, Barbie and Ken never married – all those bridal gowns were just her fantasy. 'Let's plan our dream wedding!' exclaimed the 1992 Teen Talk Barbie, who also complained that 'Math class is tough.' Although my mother had always worked (and I didn't find math class tough), I somehow ended up staking my happiness on a man – a coin toss that I lost.

During our wedding ceremony I circled the groom seven times – a Jewish tradition meant to cast a protective shield against, among other things, 'temptation and the glances of other women'. Sadly, the spell didn't work. As the details of my husband's infidelity emerged a decade into our marriage, a chapter of my life was ripped out and pulped. My brain was forced to edit the memory reel of the relationship and, with it, my very sense of self. 'Perhaps robbing someone of his or her story is the greatest betrayal of all,' says the psychiatrist Anna Fels. In her clinical experience, people who transgress have an easier time moving forward because even if they regret their choices, at least their narrative remains intact.

With my vision of the marriage shattered, I wondered what, if anything, had been sincere. Paralysed by anger, I decided to see what my favourite Buddhist teacher, Tara Brach, had to offer on forgiveness. (As she had once shared a story about a woman trying to muster loving-kindness for her ex, but finding herself wishing him a slow and painful death instead, I knew I could count on Brach to keep it real.) Releasing blame is not a one-shot deal; it's an ongoing practice. As I began incorporating Brach's forgiveness exercise into my daily meditation, on the days that 'I forgive you' stuck in my throat I mumbled, 'It's my intention to forgive you' instead. We can't will forgiveness, says Brach, but we can be willing.

In time, the protective armour encasing my heart began to soften and I was able to get on with my life. Awakening to this unplanned new reality, I felt vulnerable at first, like a newly hatched chick. Your eyes dart around, excited to discover a brand-new world, yet you're still oh-so-fragile, with bits of shell stuck to your head. As my social circle consisted predominantly of my ex-husband's friends, I found myself isolated in the aftermath, as most of our mutual friends didn't reach out at all. This turned out to be a blessing, as it forced me to make my own, more authentic friendships, but at the time it felt like yet another layer of the scaffolding of my life was collapsing.

The pain of divorce comes not only in unravelling intimacy, but in mourning the fantasy of marriage you'd been cultivating, sometimes since the days of the Barbie Dreamhouse. I had envisioned growing old together – as my parents, who were high-school sweethearts, are doing. A rupture recasts not only the story of a shared past, but an imagined future. The good news is that when I let go of the planned storyline, my life cracked open to other avenues of adventure. Since divorcing I've travelled to far-flung destinations on my bucket list, and have embarked on a writing career that gives me more profound pleasure than I had ever dreamed possible from a job. Being single offered the chance to heed the whisperings of the still, small voice that ultimately guided me to a more rewarding life.

The word 'divorce' shares a Latin root with 'divert': 'to turn in different directions'. It's painful to turn away from someone you thought was on your team. Yet it can be freeing as well. I had been so focused on the overlapping almond in the middle of our Venn diagram of interests that I ended up shelving those that weren't shared. The break-up allowed me to rediscover those pieces of myself that I had compromised, so gradually that I didn't even see them falling away. After separating, to paraphrase the poet Derek Walcott, I learned to feast on my life – revelling in doing the simplest things my way: spending a stormy Sunday reading in pyjamas; having friends over for pasta, instead of the formal dinner parties my ex enjoyed hosting; and gleefully wearing clothes he would have despised (jumpsuits!). I have cranked up the volume on myself, having muted it during my marriage.

I once asked a couples' counsellor who had been in practice for more than forty years her best advice for sustaining a long-term relationship. 'Make yourself happy,' she told me. By taking responsibility for my life since being single, I have had to forge forward myself, with no one else to blame for any unhappiness. I used to think I needed a partner's support – a personal pep squad – to bolster my self-confidence. Yet I suspect that if I'd had a boyfriend these past few years, I would have been less motivated to dig deep for the resilience to pitch ideas to editors in the face of rejection. Chances are that I would have stepped into a supporting role, rather than relying on my internal resources to realise my own ambitions.

Barbie, whose design was inspired by a German blow-up doll, was launched by Mattel in 1959. The toy was meant to allow girls to imagine their future selves rather than play at mothering baby dolls. What a limiting model of womanhood: toes perpetually on point, Barbie literally could not stand on her own two feet, not to mention the appalling lack of diversity and impossible body measurements. In a 1994 episode of *The Simpsons*, incensed by Talking Malibu Stacy saying, 'Let's buy make-up so the boys will like us!', Lisa challenges the doll-maker to make a less sexist doll. The result is the Lisa Lionheart, combining 'the common sense of Elizabeth Cady Stanton' and 'the down-to-earth good looks of Eleanor Roosevelt'. It sells a grand total of one. (There's not much of a market, alas, for down-to-earth dolls.)

In 2004 Mattel announced that Barbie and Ken had broken up; the couple rekindled their romance in 2011 on the set of *Toy Story 3*. I trust she had a ton of fun during their break. Boosted by lockdown, Barbie sales spiked by 16 per cent in 2020. I hope with all my heart that girls are coming up with better storylines than Mattel's suggestion to 'play out fabulous wedding tales and happily ever after!' for Barbie Bride. As I've got more practised at scripting my own life story, it looks more and more like a plot line I like. Whether or not a Ken wanders into my Dreamhouse, I know now that the happy ending is mine to write.

Finding Yourself Again + *Amor Fati*

NATALIE BYRNE

Trigger warning: this entry discusses sexual and physical abuse, eating disorders and self-harm.

It's easy to lose yourself in a relationship. To get lost in the magic of it all. The dream, the fairy-tale ending. To lay your head on their chest and believe everything they've said. It's OK, it happens to the best of us. I lost myself, too. Countless times; I lost myself so many times, I didn't know who the real me was.

I used to be completely addicted to relationships, jumping from one to the next. I was hooked, often thinking about my next fix while high. Sometimes there was an overlap. Often it was messy. Sometimes I was with a good guy. More often I was not with a good guy. In my relationships I have been cheated on, abused, beaten, raped and manipulated. Most of my decisions in love have been rooted in my bad relationship with my dad, and every trauma I experienced added to my baggage. This, in turn, affected my self-esteem and confidence. The way I felt about myself was already in minus, so when I faced another rejection, lie or toxic relationship I would fall further.

When I finally found peace, it was because I found myself. After my six-year relationship ended, I made a promise to myself to have a clean break from dating. I had been in relationships since I was fourteen, and I wanted to know who I was and what I wanted. I was eager to know who I was when I was no longer prioritising someone else's feelings over my own.

So I did just that. I took a year off – I called it my Man Ban. And, in 2020, I hit my two-year single anniversary. I spent those years healing, breathing and being myself, by myself. It was glorious. I can truly say now I know who I am, I'm comfortable with myself and I love myself with my whole heart.

Having discovered a lot about finding myself, I wanted to share the truths and lessons I learned with you:

Finding yourself takes time

Finding yourself is about locating your centre, what makes you unique and what your values are. This is a never-ending journey – you constantly evolve and change. Finding yourself takes time, so be patient. You will see progress gradually, but you have to do the work.

Be honest with yourself

If you find yourself repeating your mistakes and feel ready for change, start being really honest with yourself. If you find it hard to listen to your voice, intuition or gut instinct, meditation has really helped me, along with walks and making art. Quiet practices can help you pay attention to your truth and check in with what your body is telling you. In relationships I always knew when something wasn't right, but would suppress this. Accepting my truth was really difficult, but I now love spending time alone and listening to myself.

Journaling: who are you?

Journaling is an incredible healing tool. I do it every day, and whenever I want a place to rant, ramble or feel my emotions I write in my journal. Letting it out on the page is a great release for me. An activity to help you discover who you are involves making a list of what you like and what you don't like. After you've written this down, ask yourself the reason behind each like and dislike you've put down. Is what you're doing now truly meaningful to you and who you are? Getting this down on paper helped me realise how often I put my dreams, ambitions and tastes to the side and showed me what I value in my friendships and romantic relationships.

Self-acceptance

When someone rejects, judges or says something mean to you, it's important to remember this isn't about you. It's about their own insecurities, limitations and needs. Self-acceptance is about honouring where you are, right now. A journal exercise that I practise for self-acceptance is noting down what I love about myself. Try it: create a list of the things you love about yourself and add to it over time. You'll see how you change as a person, the more you find yourself; and how, alongside your growth, your likes and dislikes can change. This list also helps you to find your identity as a person outside your relationships.

Under no circumstances will you beat yourself up again

This was my crux, and the reason I self-harmed and was bulimic for so long. I punished myself for mistakes I made, but also for not seeing red flags. That you even have the capability to love, even if it's the wrong person, shows how much kindness there is inside you. It sucks that people can abuse that, especially as I've always worn my heart on my sleeve, but I try to find joy in that part of myself.

For the ones who have been cheated on

This is the best piece of advice I can give you. I had boyfriends who would always cheat on me within exactly eight months of us being together. I lived my life making decisions, picking the ones I thought wouldn't and, when they did, I would crumble. I thought I was cursed – it was all my fault, I was the common denominator. Being cheated on is some of the most painful shit I've been through, but I had an *Aha!* moment in my Man Ban, which helped me to heal and let go of the pain I had been carrying. It's not about looking for someone who you hope will never do that, although you should always walk away from any red flags. It's about knowing that, no matter what happens, you'll be OK and you have the resilience to get through it.

My Aha! moment

I had just come out of an abusive relationship when I met John.* I told him I wanted to wait to have sex and not rush into anything. If I'm completely honest, I couldn't have sex because of the abuse and the trauma I had suffered. I thought if he loved me, he would pass this test.

He went out to get us breakfast one morning and I opened his laptop to play some music. A load of messages from his ex popped up. It turned out they had been sleeping with each other the whole time. I saw it all – the sexts, everything. I cried in my flat for days, drinking a lot of alcohol and crying in my friends' laps. My best friend stayed with me in my single bed and didn't leave my side. When I woke up in the night crying, she held me. When I heard my friends discussing how shocked they were to see me this way and how they had never seen anyone in this state before, that was my first little light-bulb moment. I remember thinking, 'What do you mean? Are you saying there's another way of dealing with your emotions? Doesn't everyone react like this to heartache?' I was baffled, but also curious. This is how I saw people around me deal with pain, growing up.

The first time I went to the club, I tried to keep it together when our song came on. I cried like a baby in the smoking area, and all my friends started singing Shania Twain's 'Man! I Feel Like a Woman!' Everyone in the smoking area joined in. I remember smiling so much through the tears. When I look back on that time, it doesn't hurt any more because I remember the love I felt from my friends, holding me, having my back, cooking for me and catching

---

* A pseudonym.

me as I fell. I was so lucky to have them there for me in that moment. At the time I was so heartbroken I thought I would never love again. But I did.

I had my *Aha!* moment during my Man Ban period many years later. Spending time alone made me realise that I spent so much energy putting people through tests, instead of working on my resilience. The answer is more about you knowing that you will be fine, no matter what happens, and that you have the strength to get through anything. Trying to control any outcome – especially when it comes to another person – drove me out of my mind. It's not possible; everyone is human, and people can change their minds, fuck up and make mistakes. You can't live your life trying to protect yourself, because shit will always happen in life. The secret is building on your internal strength, so that whatever comes your way, you know you can walk away.

Just because the relationship failed doesn't mean you're a failure

Every experience you have is data. It's information, adding to your knowledge and wisdom. Use that information and carry it with you, moving forward. I know it's hard to look back on memories with someone, especially if they've mistreated you, but our past plays a vital role in who we are and who we become. I'm good at reading people now because of my past experiences. I am amazing at comforting friends through tough times, and I channel my pain into my art, turning it into something beautiful. I sometimes even make money out of my pain by bringing it into my creative practices. If that isn't making lemonade out of lemons, I don't know what is! Pain is never fun to go through, but we grow the most when we are uncomfortable.

After finding myself, I realised I wasn't asking too much. I was asking the wrong people. I found a sense of calm, because everything I ever wanted I found within myself. I found my resilience, power and inner compass. Everything I was searching for I already had within me. I simply had to find it. Spending time alone made me not only value my alone-time, but value myself. Or maybe I value my alone-time because I now value myself.

A cage can become a comfort and the wrong relationship can feel like a cage. It wasn't easy to go against everything I've been taught, to break old habits and to be out on my own. It takes courage to break the frames of tradition, or to break your patterns of behaviour. But to find who we are, we have to awaken ourselves to our truth. When we are clear on who we are and what we want, we can say yes to the things that give us meaning.

It's tough to know what healthy love is if you've grown up in a dysfunctional home, as I have. Everything started to change when I began to work on loving myself truly. At least I now have a healthy relationship with myself. And that's the most important relationship.

Everything else fell into place after I chose me: work, friends and even relationships. No one ever said, 'Damn, I regret working on myself.' If you choose yourself, I promise you it will be the best decision you ever make.

Amor fati is a Latin phrase that you can translate as 'love of your fate' or, simply, 'love of fate'. It depicts an attitude where you see everything that occurs in your life – including both suffering and loss – as being beneficial, or at least necessary.

Navigating the Seasons of Friendships as a Single Woman

NICOLA SLAWSON

'I don't know how this happened to me,' I say as my voice cracks, turning to look into the eyes of one of my best friends. 'I don't know how I ended up getting so left behind.' The words tumble out of me, even though they make me cringe. I'd just found out that of our friendship group of five, three of them are pregnant at the exact same time. The other, whom I'm speaking to now, is in a serious relationship. I'm the only one who is single. I'd already been struggling with being the only one in the group who didn't have a husband or boyfriend before this mini-break, when I find out that I am even further behind than I thought.

It's been two and a half years since that moment in a pub on the coast. The babies all arrived and are now chubby-cheeked toddlers, whom I adore with all my heart. The friend who was comforting me that day has just bought a house with her partner. Life has moved on, even for me. I am now living back in my home town and I'm much more comfortable in my single status. For the most part I'm able to shake off all the things society makes us believe about which life milestones I should have reached by now. To paraphrase Fleetwood Mac, you really can go your own way. In fact I was even recently described by the host of an acclaimed podcast as 'the poster child for single women everywhere', which that weeping girl from summer 2019 would never have believed.

Unfortunately the feeling that I'm out of sync with my friends hasn't fully gone away. This feeling is a painfully familiar one.

When I was eleven my friends refused to let me come into town with them at the weekend because I didn't have a boyfriend. They had all recently coupled up and it was an outing planned as a kind of quadruple date. Although humiliated, I protested. 'I don't mind. It will be fun anyway,' I said. They laughed. It would be too awkward apparently. Saturday came round and I sat at home with my Judy Blume book for company, wondering how I had totally missed the memo that I was supposed to get a boyfriend already. A few months later, after a period of being relentlessly bullied by the same so-called friends, I finally ditched them and found new friends, but the experience of being the odd one out has followed me ever since.

It wasn't so bad in my late teens and twenties: everyone was getting together with people and then breaking up and having periods alone. Now, in my thirties, it sometimes feels like I was too late to hop on the train with all my friends, and I'm watching from the platform as they travel further and further away from me. Meanwhile they are bonding over mortgages, dirty nappies, date nights, who takes the bin out, their child's first sentences and that time their husband did something really nice for them – and I'm still fumbling around with my ticket, not feeling quite ready to get on the same train as everyone else.

There is also the inescapable truth: I have slipped way down their list of priorities. My relationships with these women are among the most important in my life, and I would drop anything and everything if they needed me. But the fact is that it would be so much harder for them to do the same, if something happened to me. It sounds pessimistic, but while they are near the top of my list, I am further down because their babies and husbands have – rightly – overtaken me. Understanding this is one thing, but that doesn't take away from occasionally letting myself utter what I really feel about this, which is – whisper it – abandoned.

As shameful as that is to admit, I know that if the shoe was on the other foot, they would likely feel the same. I know this because I hear it so often from the single women who contact me. Like me, they don't want to feel this way, but suddenly there is a friend-shaped hole in their life that wasn't there before. They are grieving for how their friendships were. They are feeling a loss that no one is supposed to talk about. They miss their friends. And so do I.

The knowledge that I am nobody's ultimate priority can sometimes feel like a weight that sits on my chest – but it can also feel liberating and it opens up space for one of life's greatest joys: making new friends. First, a caveat: this is not about replacing my friends. I adore those women and will until the day I die. This is more about adding a few new flavours into your usual pick 'n' mix. You'll always love your old favourites (for me that's the cherries and the cola bottles, by the way), but having a few fizzy Dracula teeth just adds to the experience.

A few years ago I was temporarily living in Berlin and an acquaintance of mine set me up on a mate date with another girl who was also in Berlin at the time. I remember clearly sitting in front of this gorgeous, smart, funny woman, who had the same job as me and was also in her thirties, and immediately hitting it off. She also happened to be single. 'Jackpot,' I thought! Although we aren't as close now as she moved abroad again, she came into my life at the exact moment I needed her, and she taught me about the thrill of making friends in your thirties. It's easy to think we have enough friends, especially as life gets so busy and exhausting, but I have kept an open mind to new friends ever since meeting her.

Recently a few of my close friends have become single after break-ups, and I have also made good friends with other single people through the work that I do. Now I'm back in my home town, I'm on a mission to expand my social circle here. Although I have some absolutely lovely friends up here – some who have known me for most of my life – they are often busy with their husbands, children and full-on jobs, and I know I'll feel better when I have a couple more friends in my network to do the kind of things that make being single so awesome, like spontaneous drinks or going to midweek gigs.

Finding your tribe as a single woman is one of the most joyful things you can do – and there is power to it as well. Research tells us that when we find someone with similar experiences to our own, it validates our own experience. When the things we think or feel are normalised, it offers affirmation and actually contributes to greater emotional freedom because when we feel recognised and accepted by another, we can more easily accept ourselves.

This is not to say that the only people I hang out with now are single. Far from it. Aside from my new single friends, I have recently made new freelance friends who indulge my long voice-notes analysing what's holding me back from realising my career goals. There are also the friends who have come back into my life after a hiatus. Some had kids some time ago, but are over the sleepless nights and their children are more independent, so they have more time on their hands again. I absolutely love that we can connect over our shared history while also celebrating how we have grown during our time apart.

Having said all this, your friends getting married and having babies doesn't have to be a painful and isolating experience. It can be great. It's just hard to predict the impact it will have. In the words of Dolly Alderton, 'You can't anticipate what [babies] will do to a group of women who all love each other.' This, to me, sums up exactly what it's like to hit the period in life when people are either having babies or not having babies, and I know from the emails I get and the conversations on the Facebook group I run that many people grapple with this.

Even those who couldn't be happier to be single and child-free have to face up to the fact that many of their friends' lives are changing in ways theirs simply aren't. There is a period of adjustment. A shifting of the sands. In some cases, a total vacuum. It's impossible to predict what things will be like in the aftermath. I have close friends who have had children and, if anything, it has actually brought us closer, whereas with other friends it has put a distance between us that feels far too great to overcome.

Someone wise recently said to me, 'There are seasons in friendships that pull us apart. But there will be seasons again, where we come back together.' Maybe right now you and your best friend are in winter. It feels cooler and distant, but that doesn't mean the warmth and closeness won't come back again.

One of the things I have learned through all the highs and lows is that opening up and sharing how I feel, just like I did back in that pub all those years ago, and listening fully with an open heart in return, are two of the best tools for navigating the periods that friendships inevitably go through. Sustaining these relationships through the changing seasons can feel painful or like hard work, but if the friend is someone you don't want to let go of, then it will be worth waiting for spring to come again.

Soulmates

POORNA BELL

One of my favourite Terry Pratchett books is *Carpe Jugulum*, where he overturns the myth of a phoenix – mainly the idea that there can only ever be one at a time. 'One of anything ain't going to last very long,' says the witch Granny Weatherwax, who is also possibly the most single-by-choice character there ever was. It's how I feel about soulmates.

We are presented at a very young age with the myth that a soulmate must be romantic, and that there is only ever one of them. A perfect person designed to fit in your life like a Matryoshka doll, who knows you in a way no one else can. To ease the scepticism that might arise if you can do basic maths and are concerned about the likelihood of you meeting this individual on a planet of seven billion people, this myth is accompanied by reassuring words like 'destiny', 'fate' and 'everything happens for a reason'.

I believed in the idea of a soulmate for most of my life. First, when I was a bored teenager growing up in suburbia, listening to angsty alternative music and obsessing over boys. I am an avid diary-keeper, and the books from this time are crammed with the hopes and dreams of meeting my soulmate, and the peace, love and respite I believed I would find in doing so. Then, in my twenties, it became a more frantic thing, because now it was anchored to a timeline. It wasn't enough that I had to meet my soulmate, but that I had to do it before I turned thirty in order to keep up with the rest of my friends getting married and having children.

I kissed many toads, I placed longing and love at the feet of many men who didn't deserve it and, in doing so, I almost lost hope. We are taught, early on, that the goal is to find a vessel to pour all our love into, but nothing is said about whether the person we are giving ourselves to is worthy of our time and effort. Only that they be willing. This is not the same as mutual respect or love, and the inability to recognise that means we invest time and effort into people who may not value who we are, which can wear a person down.

Shortly after my twenty-eighth birthday, when I was about to give up on ever meeting anyone decent, I met a Kiwi man named Rob, who was introduced to me through a mutual friend. I had spent a long time being single and was so cynical about finding love that I almost didn't recognise the emotions I started to feel for him. But as we got to know each other, and that flickering spark grew into a blaze, I knew that this was different from anything I had felt before. This was all-consuming phoenix love and felt new and old, all at the same time. He was my soulmate, and it was a truth I knew as fundamentally as knowing the stars would emerge at night.

The stage was set for us to have a long life together, but the performance differed from the script I had written in my head as to what our future would look like. In 2015, after a long battle with addiction and depression, Rob took his own life. There were many things I had to contend with, but one of the hardest was: my soulmate had been snatched away from me. At the time I was only thirty-four. What did that mean for the rest of my life?

If I was to continue with the belief that you only ever get one soulmate, then the rest of life was predicted to be empty and joyless. A half-life. It was a belief that I couldn't hold on to any longer because, deep down, I knew that if I survived the grief of Rob's death, if I could get to a point where I loved being alive again, I wanted colour and laughter and fulfilment.

But also the idea that a person only gets one shot at a soulmate and that's . . . it? That isn't how nature works. Nature creates an abundance of things: different opportunities, different varieties to give the existence of any living thing, from a tree to a human, its best shot. What I eventually came to terms with is this: romantic love is not the most important kind of love by default. Sacrificing your sanity and making bad decisions in a relationship because you are pursuing some arbitrary marker of life success is not OK. While another person might feel like home, it can only ever be a resonance of what you already possess within you, unattached to another person, which is safety, peacefulness and contentment. And, finally, soulmates are not always romantic. Nowhere on Maslow's Hierarchy of Needs – the psychological pyramid of what motivates us as human beings – is there romance specifically, but rather a broader sense of love and belonging that can come from friends, family and co-workers.

This took me some time to figure out. Being a widow at thirty-four was an unusual thing, but it was also a very isolating experience. I hadn't expected to navigate being alone at this age, or mentally and emotionally cope with grief, which, back then, threatened to drown me on a daily basis. While I could relate to people in small doses when they talked about job promotions or holidays, there were parts of me that felt deadened and numb when it came to bigger milestones, such as people getting engaged or announcing they were pregnant. It wasn't that I wasn't happy for them; it was just that I couldn't relate, and our lives were so different I felt like an alien.

When I was ready to start dating again, it was almost comical how excited people got on my behalf. I knew in part that this was because it was a sign of healing, and they were happy for me, but I also believed they thought that if I met someone, maybe I wouldn't be as sad. The expectations were unrealistic: even the mention of a couple of dates was enough to set them off in a frenzy of wondering whether this could turn into something serious. I had to gently tell them that I wasn't looking for a relationship; rather I was testing the waters. While I loved Rob, it was also a relationship that had been incredibly tough at times, and I marvelled that people thought the solution to my grief lay in yet another relationship with a person, rather than focusing on the most important relationship that I had neglected over the years: the one with myself. I don't believe that you have to love yourself or fix all of your flaws before you meet someone, because emotional work is lifelong and there's no finishing line. But I do believe that you have to consider yourself worthy enough to receive love, and for some of us who put our needs last, that requires emotional growth.

Grief removes a lot of the artifice that builds up over time, like barnacles on the hull of a ship. It requires you to go into deeper uncharted waters and, in doing so, some of the things you lived your life by cannot survive the depths. What emerges from that is, in my opinion, a more truthful life. For instance, I realised that when it comes to romance, I am more of a tortoise than a mayfly. I can't slot into one relationship after another. It takes time, and things move more slowly for me. I require a lot from my connections with people, and those connections don't come along very often. Since Rob died, I have perhaps met two people I could see myself in a relationship with, but they weren't the right people in the long term. And perhaps I could have pushed it and made it work – probably at great sacrifice to myself – but something my grief has gifted me with is both the self-worth I felt from being loved by Rob and the ability to build an incredible life filled with other types of love. Both of those things combined make me more considered about who I want to be in a relationship with. And this is important, because I often feel that because domestic success is such an overwhelming sign that you've 'made it' as a woman, we've been conditioned to settle sometimes for less than we're worth.

Grief has also shifted the centre of gravity in my life. A partner is a wonderful add-on to my life, but it doesn't mean my life isn't fulfilled because I don't currently have someone. My entire life's purpose after Rob passed became about living a life that was honest and true to the person I was, rather than wallpapering it over with the expectations of others. That means a regular assessment of my life choices, from where I live to what type of jobs I take on. Some of that is really ugly work because it also involves confronting the fact that you need to let certain people in your life go. Or you have to lean into the really uncomfortable feeling of making a risky career choice, which means not knowing where your next pay cheque might come from. But you have to believe in the long-term vision, which for me is being as independent as possible.

I've been single for six years – I haven't been in a relationship since Rob passed away. To an outsider, it might appear that perhaps his death has broken me and I'm too traumatised to form an attachment. The truth is that while the kind of love and connection we had was rare, it showed me that it was possible. It showed me that I had enormous amounts of loyalty and love. But it also showed me how important it was to nurture myself and build friendships and bonds with my family members, who all pulled together to help me after he died. I realised that until that point I had lived most of my life on autopilot, and part of it in stasis, waiting for a romantic relationship to bring fullness to my life. And then, when Rob died, I was so aware of how much time I lost to grief that when I then felt able, I didn't want to waste a single minute.

What has emerged with crystal-clear clarity is that Rob wasn't the only soulmate in my life. If the definition of a soulmate is someone you connect to emotionally and spiritually in a way that seems expansive, that seems to amplify who you are and your connection to the world, then it appears that I have been gifted with an abundance. It became clear to me over the years that my first soulmate is my sister Priya, whom I speak to daily; and the second is my best friend Mal. Both of these people really see me, and truly understand me, but beyond that is the resonance we share. The closeness of the bond means that while we talk to each other all the time, a lot of our communication is unspoken, because we share a deep knowing of each other.

When I am with them, my soul feels at rest, as it did with Rob. It doesn't mean that we don't fight or disagree, or that everything is perfect. It just means that at a fundamental level I am understood and I am recognised as a person. It also means that the potential for love and connection isn't finite. It isn't a predetermined ration. The understanding that it is something that can come in many forms, through more than one person, I believe leads to a liberation of the self. It means that things are not as fixed as we believe them to be, and that means we can change the script of what we think is important.

Choosing Myself

RACHEL THOMPSON

'Give it a name,' my therapist said to me through my computer screen, her eyes narrowing in sympathy for the crying woman before her. 'I usually call it "the perfection project",' she proffered, by way of suggestion.

The perfection project was my go-to solution for coping with heartbreak. Dumped? Cool, yeah, simply change everything about yourself and then maybe, just maybe, you'll be deserving of another person's love.

My heart had been broken into pieces during the third national lockdown, and instead of doing all the things I would usually do to distract myself – brunch with friends, post-work drinks, maybe even a Hinge date – I sat on my lumpy sofa and confronted the most uncomfortable truths about myself. Such as the fact that my default mindset after something ended was to tell myself the reason he didn't want to be with me was because I needed to lose weight.

It was as regular as clockwork. The moment a situationship ended, or someone I was interested in didn't like me back, the perfection project would rear her unwelcome head. 'This is the medicine to cure all your problems, this is the road to loving yourself and being loved,' she would whisper. Her plan didn't work, though. It never did.

Disordered eating would ensue, calorie restriction became my sole activity and eventually my body would shrink. People around me would tell me I looked amazing. 'Mate, you look tiny!', 'You've lost weight, keep it up!' they would say. It always struck me as weird to hear these comments, particularly from people who knew what was going on behind the scenes. Those who knew about the pain behind the physical change. It was like winning a prize for hating yourself: 'Well done for feeling so bad about yourself that you stopped eating.' The problem was that the perfection project never made me feel any less unworthy. After the weight loss I would still feel just as unlovable. It was a big lie that left me feeling like an even emptier husk than before.

'The patriarchy has really done a number on us, huh?' a friend said to me a few years ago when I tried to articulate the battle inside me. I feel that number deep down in my bones. I've grown up with the internalised idea that I'll never be good enough for myself, let alone for anybody else.

On a Tuesday night at the end of March 2021 something happened that made me want to shake myself out of the funk I had been living in. I was looking at photographs of myself early one evening. They had been taken one year into the pandemic and my body was bigger, my face fuller. A white hotness spread throughout my body, and tears pricked the edges of my eyes. I hated the photos, but that hatred felt so normalised within me – a figure that had been lurking in the background, waiting for the right moment to jump out and reveal themselves. At that moment I realised it: I had disliked myself for twenty years. I had considered myself unlovable for two decades.

RuPaul has a saying that I used to love: 'If you can't love yourself, how in the hell are you gonna love somebody else?' Lately I've started to wonder: what if I never love myself? What if that epiphany never comes for me? Do I not get to be loved?

When this all started in my early teens I had an idea of my future grown-up self. She would be living in a city somewhere, she'd have got the hang of wearing high heels, she would hopefully be a writer and, crucially, she'd have figured out how to love herself.

Now, I am that grown-up. I'm living my dream of being a writer, I live in London and I've (just about) learned how to hobble around in heels. But loving myself? That part of me hasn't changed since I was twelve years old. And I really can't shake the feeling that by the age of thirty-two I really thought I'd have overcome this.

That's when the fear crept in. What if this is how it's always going to be in the most important relationship I have in my life – the one with myself? Am I always going to be my own worst enemy? Is my body image always going to be such an insurmountable obstacle? Am I always going to look at my friends with wonderment when they act in a way that shouts their abundant self-worth from the rooftops? Will I ever know true self-love?

What I didn't know then was that things were already changing. There was movement within, but I simply hadn't felt it yet. I had already been choosing myself time and time again. The girl I was before didn't set boundaries with the people who hurt her. They'd trample her heart and she'd lie down on the ground before them and let them do it to her again and again. When 2021 called, it was time to get up and take a stand.

At the start of the year I set a boundary with someone I still had feelings for. I was the rebound who wanted more, when he just wasn't ready. He wanted to be friends and I knew that by saying yes to this request I would be betraying myself. Deep down, I knew that a friendship would be untenable for me emotionally, and I knew that I would always want something more. Inevitably, when he moved on and found someone else, I would have to stand on the sidelines with a pretend smile on my face, acting the part of the friend who was fine with it, when in truth my heart was shattering.

In my twelfth year of being single, my thirty-second year of being alive on this Earth, I had never once set a boundary with a man. Certainly not one with whom I had seen a future, anyway. I felt a new strength, being able to walk away with my head held high, knowing I had put myself first. I hadn't set the boundary to be punitive or to hurt him in retaliation. It was an act of self-preservation, an attempt to protect myself. I was a best friend to myself in that moment.

A few months later I set another boundary with a man with the same first name as the aforementioned heartbreaker. Another man who did not see me as a romantic prospect, but wanted to carry on going out for drinks. 'It doesn't seem like the best idea, if there's no romantic spark between us,' I wrote. 'I hope that doesn't come across as harsh. I got my heart broken quite recently and need to have strict boundaries to protect myself.' He took it well, told me he understood and that it wasn't harsh at all.

Choosing myself didn't feel the way I thought it should. It did not involve me strutting in a little black dress to Beyoncé's 'Don't Hurt Yourself' while every man who ever dumped me watched on with amazement and, of course, deep, bitter regret. Although I can't deny it, this is absolutely the revenge fantasy that exists in my mind.

Choosing myself feels less glamorous than my music-video daydream. It involves hard graft. It means battling with myself and hitting the override switch when my brain tells me I could never deserve the affection of another. It requires setting boundaries with people who have hurt me, pouring my energy into the projects that will nourish me and saying no to the forces of destruction.

In this liminal space, I poured my heart and soul into writing; 40,000 words came out of me in two months. I wrote a book. I felt powerful.

The perfection project may always be there, hanging in the shadows, waiting for her moment to have her say. But just knowing that she's there means there are no surprises. The real work comes in resisting that coping strategy. My reminder is telling myself that I will not give in and I will not make myself smaller. I have believed that untruth too many times to know that it doesn't serve me well. I imagine Old Rachel standing on the other side of the canyon shouting, 'It's all a massive lie – it won't make you feel better.'

I have been single for twelve years now and, who knows, maybe I'll be single for another twelve. I look to myself as the constant in my life. The person I share every waking hour with is myself. I'm the person I consult when I need to make an important decision. Right now, that long-term relationship needs some work.

When you say the words 'love yourself' it can sound like woo-woo nonsense. But the reality of self-love isn't cookie-cutter pretty, with a bow on it. Far from it; it's messy and difficult and sometimes it honestly feels really boring and tiring. Here I go, making the most sensible decision for myself again. How utterly tedious of me!

I know one thing is for sure. I don't need to love myself fully and completely to be loved by someone else. It isn't a linear process; there will be some good days and others bad. You don't just wake up one day with a certificate that says, 'Passed: Loving Herself' before letting love in from somewhere else.

Maybe I'll love myself one day. Maybe I won't. Whatever happens, I deserve love. And I don't need to change a thing to get it.

Hot Girl Summer

RAHEL AKLILU

When twenty-six-year-old Houston rapper Megan Pete, more widely known as Megan Thee Stallion, declared it to be a 'Hot Girl Summer', nobody would be aware of the cultural phenomenon she would go on to trigger.

The 'Hot Girl Summer' meme came to represent an entire movement of self-empowerment for millennial and Gen-Z women and femmes (although the term is indeed gender-expansive and inclusive). A Hot Girl is hot, not because of society's beauty standards or expectations of what makes a 'hot' girl – but because she is confidently and unapologetically doing her own thing.

As Meg herself defines it, via her official Twitter account, 'Being a Hot Girl is about being unapologetically YOU, having fun, being confident, and living YOUR truth, being the life of the party.' In all the current talk of feminism and dismantling the patriarchy, she held a space for women to celebrate themselves and their bodies, away from the prying eyes of the male gaze or from societal expectations, that had been missing from the mainstream conversation for a long time. Meg's unabashed confidence and authenticity shone through to make her an unwitting mascot for women across the world who loved to enjoy themselves – even though she has since entered into a public relationship and declared, 'It's Hot Girl Summer but [her] man is picking her up afterwards.' Many were up in arms following her declaration, arguing that she had hijacked the movement and ruined the sentiment behind it, which got me thinking. Are being a certified hot girl and being in a relationship mutually exclusive?

I'll come back to that.

As a music journalist, the importance of a woman in rap being publicly seen to empower women is not lost on me. The frank and sometimes vulgar language prominent in rap, and lauded when used by men, is the same thing that women are villainised and criticised for, on the grounds of misogyny. The double standards mean that women can't win; they have to be sexy enough to sell records, but they can't ever acknowledge that or use it to their own advantage. Black women's bodies have been policed and exploited through every medium, for so long, that any self-expression or celebration of womanhood and sexuality has been unfairly criticised as 'a bad influence'. Furthermore, women in rap have been subject to an invisible dichotomy: on one hand, the 'conscious' musicians like Lauryn Hill who have been glorified by men for 'not taking their clothes off' (even though it's evident men haven't listened to Lauryn's lyrics properly); and on the other hand, mostly rappers, such as Miami duo City Girls or Cardi B, who have weaponised their sexuality by acknowledging it, at times mocking the world's obsession with their bodies, to ultimately profit from it. No longer do women in rap have to choose between being sexy or 'taken seriously' by the majority-male critics and tastemakers in hip-hop culture; instead they have excluded them altogether. The advent of social media has allowed women in rap to bypass the patriarchal gatekeepers and speak directly to audiences, including the women who listen to and love them.

Megan has joined a tradition of women empowering women through music, only this time she's coined the perfect catchphrase to capture the zeitgeist of the internet age. The phrase 'Hot Girl Summer' has since been co-opted by everybody from fast-food retailers to fast-fashion brands, leading Meg to trademark the phrase in 2019.

The beauty of being your unrestrained, unapologetic self and enjoying life with full confidence is what defines 'Hot Girl Summer' for a lot of women. When I ask my friends what it means, they give me answers like 'drinking margaritas by the pool', 'dancing stupidly with your friends without a care in the world' or simply 'feeling like your sexiest and most empowered self'. A recurrent theme was avoiding men, whether it was 'not letting a man disturb [my] peace' or more bluntly 'avoiding men altogether'. Absolute freedom to go where you want and wear what you like seems to be the driving force behind the appeal, untangling one's sense of self from the intricate, complicated grip of the male gaze. However, upon further introspection, I've come to find that in de-centring men from our lives, we're able to then form healthy relationships alongside individual identities. Life teaches women to centre men in how they walk, talk, dress and live. Once you do these things for your own validation, you can centre yourself and form healthy bonds with all the men in your life, free from resentment.

Outside commercial viability, how does one balance the carefree, exuberant and, at times, chaotic lifestyle of a Hot Girl with the compromise and restraint associated with relationships?

When the phrase first rose to popularity in summer 2019, my peers and I were on the cusp of adulthood, most of us finishing our undergraduate degrees and ready to let loose, before facing the world. Meg's slogan was the perfect toast, the most apt thing to shout at 2 a.m. on the night-bus home in the early hours of a balmy August morning or in the middle of choosing an outfit – for example, 'Is this dress giving Hot Girl Summer?' Meg is only a year or so older than us, and her unapologetically loud persona, as well as her candour around issues such as personal loss, relationships and body image, felt so relatable. Unafraid and witty, she felt like one of the girls we would make friends with in a basement toilet. Hot Girl Summer was ours and it was perfect.

Imagine my surprise then, when following the COVID-19 pandemic – after a year and a half of promising each other we would have the best year of our lives once we were let outside, that we would travel and enjoy and discover – the girls were nowhere to be found. All of my friends who had declared in unison with me that we were about to have 'thee' Hottest Girl Summer were now dropping like flies. A Hinge date had all of a sudden got very serious here; a rekindling with an ex during the long nights inside in lockdown there; and suddenly I was the last woman standing, with a bottle of white rum and a pink glittery cowboy hat.

'It's still a Hot Girl Summer, don't get it twisted!' they would reassure me, but almost overnight, girls' nights out (or in) clashed with romantic dates and dinners or secluded weekends away that had been pencilled into shared calendars. The 'we' that my friends used no longer referred to us, but rather to the new unit they had formed with a significant other. At the other end of the spectrum, friends who had recently come out of long-term relationships that didn't survive the pandemic were exploring 'the jungle' of singledom with the urgency of a hunting cheetah, eager to try every new dating experience that they had been sheltered from in the comfort of co-dependency. Their every move was strategic, their offhand comments serving as gentle reminders of their (completely understandable) need for recognition and desirability after time away from the psychological warfare that is dating in London.

As a twenty-three-year-old single woman with no dependants or ties, I feel as though my unattached existence has made it easier to embrace Hot Girl Summer and the notion of living my best life whilst abandoning all responsibilities – which whittles down to my choice to be single (I say 'choice' only after politely refusing a marriage proposal from a drunk man in the kebab shop once). For me, relationships of all types bring responsibility: whether it's family or friends, there is a mutual duty of care and love, the dearest responsibility being between parent and child, and that between partners coming a close second.

Already struggling to keep up with mundane things like GP appointments and balancing a full-time job in a fast-paced industry with a burgeoning freelance career, as well as a recently adopted rescue dog that has taken over my life, it's safe to say I have enough on my plate. Relationships bring love, companionship, trust and comfort. But they also bring compromise, restraint, responsibility and, to differing extents, conflict.

The freedom to do everything, or nothing, is so precious to me that the idea of sharing it or enjoying it with others hasn't, and doesn't, appeal to me. It could be my upbringing as an only child manifesting itself in my innate need for 'me time', already so scarce and precious – tucked into early-morning meditation or late-night gym sessions – but I'm at peace and truly ready to keep Hot Girl Summer alive and well, even if it's by myself.

I'm a Little Bit Jealous of My Single Friends

REBECCA REID

A couple of years ago I went to Devon with my girlfriends. I met my sister at the train station and realised, as I tried to drag my bags out of the taxi, that I was going to have to carry my own bags for the first time in half a decade.

I had to look after my own train ticket and try to work my way around M&S Simply Food for my essential train picnic (can't travel without cocktail sausages and hummus, that's the rule). My sister watched with amusement; when we finally got onto the train and I dumped my bags she said, 'You really don't know how to do anything on your own any more, do you?'

It was the kind of mean comment that only a sister can get away with, but it was also utterly true. I had become so completely absorbed into a unit of two that I didn't know how to do something as painfully simple as buying food, train tickets and boarding a train by myself.

As a couple, we have a system. He stays with the bags while I get the snacks, then I watch the bags while he buys the tickets. I carry his bag, which is always smaller and lighter. He carries mine. I always get the window seat. We didn't plan any of this, it just happened. It's like when two vines grow next to each other for so long that, to all intents and purposes, they become one plant. But while that might sound sort of romantic and nice, it's actually not. It's terrifying. Because the thing about being in a relationship is that you can pretty much instantly not be in one any more. People leave. People die. Marriages and relationships can be extinguished in the blink of an eye, and then you're landed in a world where, if you're like me and you can't navigate Waterloo station alone, you're completely fucked.

There is an odd pattern that I have observed between single women and women in relationships. We (women in relationships) seem to feel that it's our responsibility to dole out advice to our single friends. I can't count how many evenings I've sat in a garden or in a cocktail bar, giving advice (in my defence, usually advice that I've been requested to provide) about relationships. My qualification being that I am not, and at no point in the last decade have been, single.

The bar for being able to give out relationship advice is shockingly low. It doesn't really seem to matter how well your relationship functions, how much work you put into finding it or even if you're happy. If you've made it past the finish line of marriage or cohabitation, you are apparently now qualified to tell other people what to do with their lives.

I got engaged young – aged twenty-four, to be specific. And the moment that ring was on my finger, I noticed my friends treating me differently. It felt like my voice was suddenly louder, like my advice meant more. I was apparently now some kind of oracle. Of course that's completely ridiculous. I didn't get married young because I had any insight into how relationships are supposed to work. I got married young because I happened to meet, aged twenty-two, the person I wanted to be married to, and because we both wanted the same thing. It was a complete accident. Something that happened to me – not by me.

The irony is, my friends who have spent their twenties single have had the exact opposite experience. Where I mostly allowed myself to be carried through my late teens and early twenties on a tide of relationships, my single friends had to make conscious, considered choices about the lives they built for themselves. I watched as they curated their lives, choosing where to live based on what flat they liked the architecture of, or which house had a view they loved, rather than what was mutually convenient for two people's opposite-direction commutes. Their friendships with other women were deeper and more considered than mine because they spent more time together and allowed each other to be a priority. Their annual leave wasn't reserved for other people's family gatherings and a one-couple holiday. Their weekends were for friends and hobbies, and time spent peacefully alone. My diary, by contrast, looked like one of those police whiteboards where they're trying to solve a murder, attempting to balance our respective friends, family, exercise, cleaning and food-shopping commitments.

My friends who were single throughout their twenties had spent their time reflecting on who they were, what they really wanted, and on having and holding things they loved. While I had tried to do the same thing, I could never have managed that same level of self-reflection or self-reliance.

The best-case scenario for me now is that I will never live alone – or at least that I will only ever do so very late in life, a sweet old widow with a cottage by the sea. I'm unlikely to travel the world by myself, to take a job abroad, to have any significant solo adventures. If I do ever find myself in that position, it will be because I have lost something in a catastrophic way.

I can't help having a tiny shred of envy for those women who will reach a long-term relationship (or choose to remain single long-term) having already spent some years getting to know themselves. I've heard so many of the women I love lamenting their single status, paraphrasing the moment in *Sex and the City* where Charlotte wails, 'I've been dating since I was fifteen, where is he?' And while I don't say it, because I don't think it would be helpful, I want to tell these friends that when they do eventually find 'the one', they're going to be in the best position of all because, unlike me, they won't have skipped an entire chapter of personal development.

I realised, after that day at Waterloo station, that I'd spent years working on my relationship with my husband and roughly ten minutes working on my relationship with myself. Then the pandemic hit, and things only got worse. For months on end I was in isolation with just one person for company. By the start of 2021 I knew I needed to make some changes. I resolved to invert the relationship I had with my single friends. Instead of being the Grandmother

Willow figure, doling out advice that I had no real authority to give, I started to listen. I observed what my friends who were self-reliant and non-co-dependent were doing, and I tried to emulate it.

Every week, on a Sunday morning, I went to a ballet class in Central London by myself. I stole back a portion of the week to do something I loved before I was in a relationship. Taking a bit of Sunday – the most coupley of days – felt like a very small but significant rebellion. After class, I would often go and have a cup of coffee at the deli around the corner and watch huge Italian families with their *bambini* streaming out of church. I might walk home sometimes, or stop by a gallery on the way home. Sometimes I would get my eyebrows done or have a manicure. It didn't really matter what the activity was. What mattered was that I was doing it alone, and instead of forcing my time with myself into the crevices of the week, I was putting 'me' on par with 'us', by allowing myself some time alone at the weekend. I didn't let myself rush home, or feel guilty for using up time that could be spent together on being alone. It probably shouldn't have been surprising to discover that, ironically, this carving out of a little more space in my marriage actually made things work rather better, as well as making me feel more like a person in my own right.

It would be disingenuous to pretend that I have cured myself of my co-dependency. But I'm trying to do better. I carry my own ticket when I travel. I've got a wheelie suitcase, which I can whizz around Marks & Spencer in seconds. I have lofty ambitions for a trip to Paris by myself next year, and I have stopped permitting myself to turn down invitations because it's a girls-only event, or because it's on a Sunday. Most of all, I've realised that when I spend time with my single friends I need to expend as much time on receive as on transmit, because being married or finding a long-term partner doesn't mean that you've cracked it.

All of the self-improvement that people go through while looking for a partner is just as important if you're married or settled down. And while it might be harder to come by when you're one half of a couple, it's still perfectly possible, if you're willing to carve out a little bit of singledom inside your relationship.

There Is Nothing to Fear

ROSE STOKES

The door closed in front of me. On one side was a relationship that had crumbled into dust, on the other side was me, twenty-nine, freshly uncoupled and completely fucking terrified. Palms sweaty, breathing shallow, vision blurred – these were the only sensations I remember feeling in the first few moments of what turned out to be the most enlightening years of my life.

It would be fair to say that before that moment I had never considered why I was so afraid of being single. It is the state in which I entered the world and is how I will leave it, and yet, somewhere along the path from childhood to adulthood, it has become a source of shame. Instead of finding my new single status calming, after months of chaos and intense anxiety provoked by being in an unhealthy relationship, I felt fear. The hot, sweaty, panicky kind of fear that throws everything into uncertainty and makes you doubt your value as a person.

Where did I learn it, this fear? It hadn't always been there and yet here it was, urgent and bubbling, asking for answers to a well of questions that I didn't even know had been long lingering inside me. Would I be alone for ever? What did my inability to remain attached to someone say about me as a person? About my value? How would I get used to doing things alone again? What would people think of me? What did I think of myself?

I didn't know how to be alone, not really. Not in the truest sense of the word. The previous spells that I'd spent single had been ruled by a fervent desire to 'solve' my single status – to 'correct' it and make myself more socially palatable by finding a partner. And if that wasn't possible, to present myself at least as being on the lookout.

The constant pressure to find someone to settle down with made it hard to relax into my singleness, so trained was I to be constantly alert to the presence of any potential match. It's stupid, when I think about it now, how social conditioning builds up our distaste of singleness as a lifestyle choice, when actually being in a bad relationship is so much worse than anything I've ever experienced being on my own.

'This is a good thing,' my best friend said encouragingly over the phone, 'you're clearing space for something better.' I wanted to believe it, but I just couldn't. It felt like a lie. Like the sort of thing you tell yourself to feel better. Like a denial of what was really happening, because I was so certain that I was destined always to be alone.

Despite the fact that my relationship had been a complete and utter disaster – and that leaving it was an objectively Good Thing – I couldn't shake the notion that I was a failure for letting go. For not making it work. For prioritising my mental well-being rather than my relationship status. I wanted to believe that both could be true: that being single and being happy could coexist. But how could I, when every time I looked around in social circles, on TV, in magazines, all I was presented with was happy couples, and single people trying desperately not to be?

'And why do you think it is,' my therapist asked me one day, not long after we began to meet, 'that you are so very afraid of being alone?' The air between us felt charged all of a sudden.

'Isn't everyone?' I shot back, perplexed.

'I asked about you,' she responded calmly.

In all our excavation of my recent break-up, the question of why I had stayed so long is the part I had struggled most to understand. But as I poked and prodded this feeling sitting somewhere an inch or two behind my belly button, beliefs and ideas started to pour out of me.

For as long as I could remember, I'd been obsessed with the relationship status of people that I met or people I saw on TV. 'Do they have a partner?' I'd ask my friends if ever they mentioned a new person, so fascinated was I by the relationship status of others.

I'd google celebrities I liked and trawl through their relationship history, desperately seeking validation of my own. Sometimes the situation would call for me to be more direct. 'Who are you going on holiday with?' I'd ask colleagues as they signed off before annual leave, desperate to know if they were one of the coupled-up ones or if we were the same.

Along with this interest came a certain sense of veneration for those who were coupled. 'They must be great,' I'd think, regardless of any obvious personality traits or characteristics that might suggest otherwise, for someone else to endorse them with their love. It was a great marker of success, to my mind: the ability to sustain a relationship. Were they happy? I didn't really think about it, assuming that by virtue of being in a couple, they must be. Isn't that what we were all aiming for, us humans?

An experience common to all of those people who identify as a woman is that we are taught to value ourselves by our sexual attractiveness. Perhaps that was really at the core of my fear. Maybe what I was afraid of was that, without the presence of someone offering proof of my value by formally agreeing to have sex with me every now and then, I didn't have any value at all. But when I created space inside myself that truly belonged to me, and let myself enter it and look around, what I really found was a million different opportunities to value myself that had nothing to do with the way I look, my desirability or the ways in which others related to me.

It seems incredibly naïve to think back on it now, the way I rarely questioned whether or not being happy was more important than being attached. But then again, my worldview was – and still is – very much supported by the society in which we live. There were social structures underpinning the way I felt about my relationship status, and encouraging me to believe that being single was something to be feared or, at the very least, to be ardently avoided. Our obsession with relationships is so culturally engrained that we choose to celebrate the union of two people and commiserate with break-ups, regardless of the circumstances. We've learned to understand that happily ever after at the end of a film means two people getting together – even our tax system is set up to make it easier (and cheaper) for those living in pairs to exist. Maybe it would make more sense to ask: why would I ever have questioned it?

Years passed and I grew more comfortable in my solitude. Over time, I began to notice a little thought creep in every now and then as I watched yet another person close to me find their mate, an occasion that I would historically have used to lambast myself for being single. Maybe ... Maybe it didn't have to be this way? Maybe my value as a person didn't have anything to do with whether or not someone chose to share a bed and a bank account with me. Maybe without the layer of social cushioning that a relationship afforded me, I could do something truly novel and endorse myself for once?

'What a mad concept,' I'd quickly think, pushing all of these bright little sparks back into the dark corners of my mind. But it didn't stop them returning and, over the years that followed, they began to appear with greater frequency – a bit shinier each time and harder to extinguish.

I'm going to resist the urge to give you a neat little narrative documenting my perfect transition into contented single liberation. To tell you that I stopped longing for a partner, or began to see myself as truly whole on my own. I wish I could. I'd love to, in truth. But it wasn't quite like that. The reality was much messier – and much more beautiful for it.

In increments, life did become easier. Being alone became easier. The more time I spent on my own, the more I began to crave it. The more I invested in improving the quality of time that I spent alone, the more I enjoyed it. The more I began to believe that I deserved the same compassion I so readily gave out to others, the more I leaned into my solitude. I began to proactively seek out examples of happy women who had eschewed a life coupled up, in search of something else, and make them my role models instead. When friends or family members asked if there was anyone special in my life, I gradually became more comfortable saying no and resisted the urge to explain what I was doing to correct this. I interrogated where I'd inherited the idea that I wasn't enough on my own, and questioned its legitimacy more frequently (though not always, of course). I looked around me at the couples I knew and took off my rose-tinted glasses for long enough to see that their lives weren't richer or better than mine, they were just different. Eventually I began to believe – to really, deeply believe – that maybe whatever happened, I would be OK. Only then did I know there was nothing to fear in being alone, although I still have to remind myself of this every so often.

Living without fear of being single helped me to make better decisions, too. Why would I put up with the bad behaviour of people within the context of dating when I was so happy on my own? What I learned is that fear doesn't necessarily have to deter us from the path ahead of us. Only by leaning into it do we become braver and understand new facets of ourselves. For me, at least, the years I've spent alone have been the most instructive and the most enlightening. They have enabled me to articulate my wants and needs better with new partners, without worrying that I'd lose them if this didn't tally up with their own expectations – and so the quality of my partnerships has improved, too. Without time alone to really understand all of this, and to move away from fear and into empowerment, I'm not sure I'd ever have understood how to make myself truly happy.

Four years have passed since I slammed that door and, by hazard or coincidence, I have met someone I like. He is charming, kind and attentive, and I feel safe when I'm with him. A pandemic looms large in our peripheries, forcing conversations that we might have preferred not to have until much later on.

'I like you and I want to commit to this,' I begin to type. 'But if you're not ready for that, I completely understand.' I stop and take a deep breath, swallowing back the pangs of a familiar fear. 'The thing is, I'm happy on my own. So if you like me too and want to see what this could be, then let's do it. But if not, I know I'll be OK.'

I press send, put down my phone and go for a walk.

The Golden Days

ROSIE WILBY

One bright autumn morning during the unravelling of my five-year relationship I strolled briskly from our rented house on Brixton Hill across Brockwell Park to the Lido. I was looking forward to the mindful back-and-forth of swimming lengths. It was my daily therapy, clearing my mind of my feelings of fear and hurt. Although my girlfriend and I were separating as compassionately and amicably as possible, in something of a 'conscious uncoupling' model, I was starkly aware of how much I would miss her steadfast companionship.

Yet on this particular morning I felt a new sense of calm wash over me. I was listening to a sort of 'break-up playlist' on my clunky iPod, an outdated model that my girlfriend often gently mocked. As I turned up the concrete path towards the tennis courts, Richard Hawley's yearning song 'Open Up Your Door' started up. As the strings began to swell, I noticed some golden leaves trapped in the criss-cross intersections of the wire fencing. There was something about the way they glinted in the shafts of hazy sunshine that made me pause. They were hardly Wordsworth's daffodils. But there was something about the way they hung there, soon to decay, yet still beautiful. They seemed like memories of old love, little trophies to be celebrated, not mourned.

As much as a chapter of my life was ending, a new chapter was beginning, too. I was about to be single. And that, I realised, was going to be just fine.

My comedian friend Juliet Meyers describes a similar musically-triggered moment of awakening as the embers of her last relationship slowly turned to dust a decade ago. While she waited in the wings before stepping onstage at a gig, the drag-queen compère launched into an unexpectedly moving rendition of The Beautiful South song 'I'll Sail This Ship Alone'. Juliet, in a mixture of terror and excitement, immediately thought to herself, 'That's what I'm going to do. I'm going to sail my ship alone. I'll spend more time on my comedy, more time travelling and on all of the things that I love.' She realised that she had compromised so much during the cosiness of commitment that she had lost sight of herself. She has revelled in single life ever since.

When we emerge from a relationship we have often been stuck, run aground, for a while. Yet we are suddenly, perhaps unexpectedly, experiencing music and colour with a new intensity, observing our life from a new vantage point. And we have the autonomous freedom to determine which way to turn next. Hurting and confused as we may be, there's a peculiar energy about us at this transformative moment of renewal. These primal feelings that can sometimes push us towards destructive acts of revenge can instead be harnessed and used as forces for good, for creativity, for moving forward towards new adventures and connections. I call it 'break-up energy'.

In fact a 2003 study published in the academic journal *Personal Relationships* and co-authored by writer and speaker Ty Tashiro and Patricia Frazer found that a group of ninety-two undergraduates who had experienced a recent romantic break-up reported, on average, five positive types of personal growth that they thought might improve their future romantic relationships. These ranged from boosted self-confidence to learning how to be a better partner and, perhaps most crucially of all, how to choose a better partner, too. Women reported more growth than men did.

Journalist and author Helen Croydon thinks that we often seek out activities and pursuits in a newly single life that are the opposite of some of the things we ended up resenting doing while in a relationship. When her partnership with a pub-loving 'bon viveur' ended, she found herself propelled into doing something more worthwhile with her weekends. She joined her local running club, entered the London Triathlon, kept up a gruelling training regime through the mud, rain and snow and eventually qualified for the World Championships.

Meanwhile, countless comedians have come up with their best work in the wake of a separation. John Robins and Sara Pascoe both wrote about their 2016 Christmas break-up in their 2017 Edinburgh Fringe shows. He went on to win the Edinburgh Comedy Award for *The Darkness of Robins*, in which he pedantically found comfort in the tiny victories of newly single life (a single person's council-tax discount and knowing where the iPhone charger cable is), and she had five-star reviews for her show *LadsLadsLads*, in part inspired by an awful break-up recovery yoga-retreat in Costa Rica.

Perhaps similarly, I have often found myself feeling way more capable and brave when there's suddenly no partner to lean on for help. It is during my times spent single that I have really challenged myself and got shit done. I transformed myself from an introverted bedsit songwriter, who rarely dared to set foot out of the house, into a stand-up comedian, speaker and podcaster who has travelled the world and has something to say (on a good day anyway). Ironically, the safety net of having a partner around had always squashed my ability to take the giant, risky leap into free fall that I so desperately needed.

I have often puzzled over the curious cultural binary that seems to value coupledom over singledom. The truth that I have experienced is the exact inverse of this – a photo negative of our programmed expectation. Film director Yorgos Lanthimos also comments on it in his bizarre and biting 2015 satire *The Lobster*. The characters who play by the rules and pair off get to stay in a luxury hotel, while the rebels and renegades who opt for single life live as outcasts in the woods, facing the lashing wind, rain and storms. Yet a more genuine kind of connection seems ultimately more likely to blossom out there in the real world than in a high-pressure production line of forced matches. Maybe it is during these times spent single, facing the crashing waves of self-reflection, that we are free to be at our most authentic and electrified. And to become a bigger, better version of ourselves to take into a relationship again, if we so choose.

And it is this matter of choice that is so vital. Ever since I came out as a lesbian at the tender age of nineteen, I have been painfully aware that there are, in pure statistical terms, way fewer potential love interests out there than there might have been, had I been straight. In dating-app terminology, gay people are what is known as a 'thin market'. Try switching your Tinder feed to women and not reaching the 'There's nobody new around you' message. During my twenties and thirties I scurried and hurried into relationships just because the person seemed nice and normal . . . and was gay. 'Hallelujah. I'd better marry them immediately,' I thought every time (even though technically that wasn't legal yet). There was no robust analysis of whether we were actually compatible; only attraction and blind hope.

Yet when I became single in my forties, after that gloriously golden moment in Brockwell Park, it was clear that a major cultural shift had happened. Being single had emerged as a stigma-free and socially valid option for women of all sexualities. Words like 'spinster' had been banished. I felt, for the first time, that I could take my time. Dating might actually be fun rather than a manic headlong sprint. If there wasn't anyone available who was good enough to commit to, I could wait until there was. I had never really experienced that before. I felt a new sense of control.

This new feeling allowed me to make a better choice. Four years ago I met my fiancée. We live together in South London with our dog and two cats. There are certainly days when I think back wistfully to my single days or even glance enviously at the freedom that single friends seem to enjoy. Yet I know that everything I learned during those times is still there under the surface.

Perhaps we should not get so hung up on the beginnings of relationships, thrilling and exciting as they are. Surely beginnings of new love are also endings of a period of singledom and of intensely active personal growth? And perhaps it is these endings, these 'break-ups', that we should be the most alert to, and that we should navigate the most consciously of all. Don't abandon your singlehood lightly. It can be a very precious and shining gift.

A Single Woman Is the Closest Living Thing to a Goddess

SALMA EL-WARDANY

Once upon a time, in a land far, far away, a girl was born. She grew up beautiful and sweet, met a charming man, got married and then we never heard about her again because she was no longer relevant or useful to society. The husband lived Happily Ever After and she lived a life of housework, child-rearing and turning herself inside and out to be the perfect wife and mother, which is to say, she lived Exhausted Ever After.

The first part of that story is the one we spoon-feed to girls the minute they pop out of the womb, swaddling them in pink Baby-gros while telling them that one day their prince will come for them. If it's not Disney peddling that story, it's some auntie down the local mosque/church/synagogue reinforcing it by continuously asking young women when they're going to get married.

The second part of that story is the one we don't tell. That's why all the fairy tales and rom-coms end when they get married; if the story were to continue, perhaps we wouldn't be able to get women down the aisle in the first place. Because it's a truth universally acknowledged by all women that men, marriage and motherhood is an absolutely exhausting, draining and tiring endeavour. But we don't talk about that. The realities of maintaining a relationship, household and family are still brushed under the carpet and hidden behind closed doors while we continue to tell women that coupling up with a man is the only way to live.

It's a tale I bought into myself, despite my feminist protestations. As a young girl I'd planned, in great detail, the type of wedding

I wanted. In my mind, it was a grand affair that would take place in the castle where Harry Potter was filmed. The theme would be black and white, my dress would be a corset-waist with a skirt so big that a castle was the only viable venue for it, and the wedding favours absolutely would not contain anything with raisins in. I'd given greater thought to this wedding than I had to the man who would be waiting at the end of the aisle. I'd laid out my demands for this day before I ever demanded what I wanted in a relationship or expected from a man. When I fell in love, I merely continued to add details to the elaborate wedding plan, which had started before I knew the name that would be on the invitations next to mine.

Two relationships, one situationship, a f*ckboy and a broken heart later, I found myself single, financially independent and living alone, which was never something I'd planned. I didn't play-act being single as a girl, I never dreamed about living alone and not once did I google 'single-girl house inspo' for ideas of what my home, or life, would look like without a man in it. I didn't talk to my girlfriends about being single, and no one, not once, told me this was a viable path for me in life.

The truth is, we only talk about single ladies when we're dancing to a Beyoncé track. When the music is loud enough to drown out the fear of loneliness, and when the sweat dripping down your face makes you feel like you're shining. When the men, for once, know their place and have stepped off the dance floor and you're free to move your body to the music without the threat of a grope or a grab under the guise of 'we were just dancing'. When you're surrounded by other single women and the adrenaline is flowing fast enough to make you believe you can change the world. When the married women with their talk of nappies and night-feeds, which you normally smile politely and nod at, have taken a seat on the sidelines and, for once, the single women are celebrated. For three minutes and twelve seconds, single women are spoken about outside the parameters of 'spinsters', 'old maids' and 'lonely women'.

The lack of conversation and celebration around single women is one of the most dangerous disservices we do to women and girls. We are in dire need of an overthrow of Hollywood's romance – in favour of something far more satisfying than a sub-par kiss at the end of a movie from a man who's suddenly realised that he can't live without her, even though she'd realised all along but, as usual, had to wait for the man to mess up before catching up. Instead of flogging marriages and men, we should be teaching essential singledom. We should encourage women to aspire to single status, because being single for a prolonged period of time is one of the most radical acts of feminism a woman can do.

While my seven single years happened entirely by accident, they were some of the sweetest years of my life. They taught me some of the most valuable lessons of my life. I learned how to make my own money and thrive off it. How to get on a plane and travel the world by myself. How to take my pleasure when and where I wanted it. How to love myself wildly because most nights there wasn't anyone else to do it and it would drive you wild if you didn't. How to carry the shopping home after a fourteen-hour day at the office. How to fill my vases with my own flowers. How to pay the rent and the taxman by myself because there was never anyone else to split it with. How to take the apologies out of my mouth and how to say, 'Here, this is what I want.'

All of this is not to say that I don't believe in love and marriage; however, what I am saying is that during my single years I made a woman who never would have been forged in the shadow of a man. Liking and loving a man, in a world that was built for men by men, is a fundamentally unequal partnership.

Historically women were 'given' by fathers to husbands. Matrimony was an alliance between tribes, nations and families. Women often entered into marriages with men they hated, for economic safety and to avoid a life of destitute poverty. The very structure of the patriarchy has so effectively disempowered women that binding your life to a man, who enjoyed economic wealth and social freedom, was often the only means of survival. While the argument now is that times have changed and women enjoy far greater liberation without the need to marry for survival – and while that may be true in some places, but not all – that doesn't mean the patriarchy has been disabled. It thrives today just as well as it always has because the structure of our society remains a deeply patriarchal one.

We still don't educate boys and men about consent and female bodies. We don't require communication and emotional intelligence from them. We don't ask men to stay at home and raise children while the women go out to work. We still live in a world in which men are unable to communicate and process their own emotions. In short, we exist in a world in which the bar for men is so low that we believe we've found 'a great guy' if he puts a condom on before sex without being asked. That is the reality of our gender relations and so, while I believe in marriage and love, I also believe that to have a successful partnership with a man, he has to be prepared to throw off the shackles of patriarchy, understand feminist theory, dismantle his own toxic masculinity and do about ten years of therapy before he's ready to be with a woman. And because the pull of patriarchy is so powerful, even when you happen upon such a man, it still takes an enormous amount of awareness, effort and emotional labour to resist yielding to a man and acting out traditional gender roles.

Which is exactly why the single years matter so much. They teach us how to say no. How to speak up and ask for what we need. How to walk away from situations that don't serve us. They teach us how to be so gloriously happy alone that it takes someone remarkable (for example, a man who has done the work, which is a remarkable feat in itself) to tear you away from yourself.

During my single years I met a man who once told me that I was the closest living thing to a goddess he'd ever met. Not because he found me attractive or because of my physical appearance, but because I lived alone, had money to spend and always demanded what I wanted. I thought about that long after he left my house and we'd stopped sleeping together. If I am a goddess, it's only because the single years have taught me how to be so. I think all the single women look like goddesses to me. They take their pleasure from lovers and friends and rise the next day to earn the money. They keep the roofs on and the cupboards full. They put bread on the table and money in their bank. Their mouths have lost the taste of apologies. They are powerful and unafraid, and that in itself is fearful to a social structure built on women being dependent on men and the economy of men. Perhaps this is why they never wanted us to be single in the first place. They'd rather keep us dependent, tied up, with our wealth in the shared account. To be single, independent, hungry and unapologetic is to be the closest living thing to a goddess.

The Hamster Wheel

SHANI SILVER

We think of being single as limitation, as lack. As if life is holding us back from fully living it. Don't feel bad – we were groomed to think this way, it's fine. We've always seen these charming perks of being in a couple that we, as singles, never have access to. Things like celebrations, a designated plus one for concerts and travels, really nice kitchen appliances, and so forth. The number of things we think we can't do while we're single is astounding, especially when you also realise that every single one of these can't-dos and can't-haves is a giant, festering lie. As far as singlehood goes, nothing actually holds us back like societal norms.

There are certain social conventions that we think we have to abide by. This happens very naturally because we've been abiding by these rules since we were first educated on the importance of obeying traffic signs and resisting the urge to put one's elbows on the table. We've been well trained. So it doesn't shock me that there are societal expectations holding single people back from living their singlehood fully, if not loving their singlehood so much that they won't let it go for anything other than the right relationships. Did you think this would be another epic rant about the perils of being single? Tuck in, my friends, we're going to have a good time together.

It might be strange for a single person to hear that something about their singlehood isn't their fault. Believe me, I know how used to the opposite scenario we truly are. The society that we so badly want to fit into loves to make us feel like our singlehood is shameful, and that we're causing it with all our terrible, terrible flaws. But with regard to staying stuck and small in our singlehood because we're waiting for the 'permission' of a relationship to allow our 'real' lives to begin, it's not actually something we do to ourselves. It's something we believe, because it's what we've been taught.

It's a bit of a hangover from childhood perhaps – the idea that we have to wait for permission from other people to do the things we want to do. Personally, I've come to a place in my life where I can't be bothered to wait for permission. I have too many things I'd like to do, and I shouldn't have to wait for a wedding registry to own a fancy blender – let's cut the nonsense and get moving.

The societal norm that I believe is most harmful to single women is this: you either have to pursue a relationship with the fervour and determination of a racehorse or 'swear off' dating completely and 'choose' to be single for ever. It's one or the other. Exhaust yourself to the brink of madness by dating, or claim solitude as a defence against it. Societal norms haven't shown us that there's any other story. There aren't other ways to be single. You either date, date, date, date, or you're a spinster who doesn't believe in love. It certainly hasn't shown us that there's an entire singlehood spectrum we get to operate within, and that the vast majority of that spectrum doesn't suck.

You don't have to make dating the centre of your single life. Did you know that? That you're allowed to have more balance? Our lives contain a multitude of focal points beyond our careers. Some of us garden, others throw pottery; maybe we enjoy athletics, or perhaps we sing. (I do not sing, as I'd prefer not to summon all local howling dogs, hyenas and demons to my current location.) We spend our non-working time in so many different ways, but when we're single, nothing claims the focus like dating. Dating hoards the majority share of our attention, effort and concern. It's an implied chore that applies to single life. If you're single, you don't have a relationship, and that's bad, so you date! It's very passive and accepted – nothing strange about it.

Until you date, and then date more, and you try, and then try something else, and you do everything society tells you to, and give everything you have to this endless, maddening effort. Societal norms tell us that if we're single, we have to date until we find someone. But where is society when all that dating doesn't actually lead to someone? Will society and its norms comfort us, take care of us or – imagine it – actually introduce us to this person it's shaming us to find? No. Society has no comfort for spent singles, just more shame, pity and sadness. And the only solutions that we, as singles, have looked into yet are continuing to endure a punishing dating culture or giving up entirely.

A truly important thing to understand about being single and actively dating is that dating is one area of life where effort doesn't match reward. If you want to learn a new language, you study, and then you know a new language. If you want to bake a cake, you mix the ingredients, bake and enjoy. But not in the dating space. You can put all the effort you want into 'finding someone', but dating never has to deliver. It knows we'll keep devoting ourselves to it all the same – because we've been so societally conditioned to believe that being single is bad. Funny, I've been the happiest I've ever been since I de-centred dating from my life. You know what I really think? I think dating culture is the miserable thing, not singlehood – and it's been letting singlehood take the blame for its crimes this entire time.

The amount of work (and suffering) we put into dating never, ever has to result in meeting our partners. It might, but it never has to. We're not in an equation, we're in a hamster wheel. It's that 'might', and that 'maybe', that keeps us going. Dating culture, and certainly dating apps that profit off the shame of singlehood, never have to give you what you're looking for, but they get to take advantage of your hope all the same. You are just as likely to meet your partner in the fifth person you go out with as in the 500th. The effort we put into dating doesn't have to balance out with the resulting partner we think should be here by now. And since dating culture doesn't keep things balanced for singles, we have to take matters into our own hearts. Yes, I know that sounds cheesy, but stay with me.

There's more balance to be had for singles. It is possible to be open to, and desire, a relationship while also not making dating the focal point of your life. It's possible to stop giving so much of your energy to dating and still meet someone anyway. There's a broad range of options and ways of living in between a miserable, exhausting singlehood and deciding to be single for ever. That's not a choice we actually have to make as singles in order to be considered valid. Our singlehood is valid any way we choose to live it. You don't have to drain yourself in the dating space to feel like you're 'doing enough' to end your singlehood. There's no possible way to 'do enough' and, honestly, singlehood isn't that abhorrent.

We need reminders of all the ways people have come together. I know that 'how we met' stories are a bit of a brunch eye-roll for singles, as they're societally predisposed to spark jealousy. But what if instead of becoming jealous, we allowed stories of how people met to broaden our minds? What if these stories served as reminders of the infinite number of ways people meet and fall in love? Wouldn't that allow us to release the vice-like grip we have on our apps and our commitment to dating and let us just . . . I don't know, live?

People meet at work. They meet at conferences. They meet on planes, trains and buses. They meet through friends, they meet at bars. They meet on the actual street sometimes. It's endless, and if there are endless ways people come together, maybe that knowledge can help single people let go a bit. Maybe we're not as in control as we thought we were, and maybe that's OK. Maybe we can't force a relationship to happen, and maybe we wouldn't want a relationship that we had to force in the first place.

I know that putting less effort into dating sounds terrifying, because we associate that reduction in effort with an increase in the amount of time we'll be single. But we're allowed to recognise that those two things aren't correlated at all. Relationships happen, love happens. We can't control, plan or cause these things with all of our toiling away in the dating space. So maybe we can let go and acknowledge that we're allowed to simply live, to just be, and connect with beautiful relationships that are meant for us when they're meant to happen. Something else is allowed to happen, too. We're allowed to love being single. We're allowed to value this time in our lives for all its freedom and possibility. We're allowed to stop spinning our wheels, and start loving our lives. That doesn't sound like giving up, to me.

Stepping Off the Rollercoaster

SHAPARAK KHORSANDI

In my teens and early adulthood I had no clue how to connect with guys. I'd watch other girls hanging out with them, laughing, flirting and often actually dancing with them, seemingly unself-conscious. They would be friends with them, sleep with them, have relationships with them, while I never understood why hanging out with some hot bloke could, on any planet, be more fun than hanging out with your mates. If I ever talked to a guy I actually fancied, I could in no way be myself. I was clunky and awkward and there would be a bogey up my nose. At least I was sure there was, so I'd mumble something inappropriate before wandering off to find that my nose was crystal-clear, yet I was dying of embarrassment regardless.

I was so clueless about the intensity of sex and relationships that at university, when a mate's boyfriend from home came to visit her, I sat in her room drinking wine and eating crisps, completely oblivious to the looks they were giving each other that said, 'When is she going to leave?' I didn't lose my virginity until I was almost twenty-one. I had no idea that sex was more fun than listening to my hilarious takes on everything. At one point I said, 'Hey! Why don't I grab a sleeping bag and we can have a slumber party!' Steam was coming out of her boyfriend's nose as she delicately explained that they wanted to be alone. As I gathered my things and shuffled off, I thought about how I'd been about do my Orville impression for them. They must really like sex to miss that.

I am currently forty-eight and, after all these years, I'm finally comfortable with the fact that I was right first time: I don't want to be in a pair. The world is chock-full of messages of who I should be and what I should do to achieve this.

'Find a man, settle down.'

Some of us don't want to 'settle'. If you find a partner you are deeply in love with and want to journey through life with, then my goodness that is beautiful and someone ought to write a song about it. 'Settling', though? Nope. Never again.

My journey to accepting that I need to be single, to focus on what's best for me, was a long one. I eventually had encounters with guys, but they were drunken, awkward and usually only worth the stories I'd tell my friends later over drinks, sharing every detail (apart from the one where I felt massively rejected when he didn't arrange to see me again) as we laughed our heads off. Or I'd feel awful because I hadn't wanted it to happen at all and there had been no part of it I'd enjoyed. I'd get hopelessly fixated on guys who were totally unavailable to me, and the men I did actually go out with for a while in my early twenties – never for more than a few months – I wasn't all that into, and I would always much rather be with my friends than with them.

However, at the age of twenty-three I fell in love. For the first time there was a human being I was with that I couldn't get enough of. Someone I wanted to learn every detail about. He was much older than me and I loved him deeply. He drank, though. A lot. The two of us drank together for several years until I realised that all I had to show for it, if we continued, would be several skips full of empty Lambrusco bottles. I never stopped loving him and it was a hammer-blow when he died in early 2021.

Booze was a huge part of my twenties and thirties. It was easy to bury myself in it under the guise of 'having fun!' It was, after all, the nineties and any attempt towards self-care and self-soothing was reserved for the hippies at the Healing Field at Glastonbury.

Booze and a bewilderingly low self-esteem led me to date men who really weren't right for me. They weren't all bad people, some were simply not right for me. Astoundingly, I never considered myself in all of it – what I wanted, needed or valued. I had one-night stands, which filled me with shame and regret. There were nights when I definitely did not consent, but they do not count in this list of 'inappropriate liaisons'.

I married a man who didn't love me. I went out with a guy who cheated on me while I was at home with my son. I went out with guys who failed to mention they already had a girlfriend, even when asked directly. I had a second child with a man who left me five seconds (I counted them) after I showed him the little stick I had weed on. I dated men who were younger than me who didn't understand how hard it was to work and raise my kids and be a doting girlfriend. I went out with older men, but they didn't seem to understand this, either.

This continued right into my mid-forties. I was a serial monogamer and you'd have thought that, throughout all this, I might, just once, have had a healthy, balanced relationship by accident, but it never really happened. It took a diagnosis of ADHD when I was forty-four to make me realise that the common denominator in these massively troublesome relationships was me.

For decades I had mistaken romance and adrenaline for love. I spent years of my life fixated on the impossible task of untangling endless drama within toxic unions. So skewed was my focus that I actually believed the drama would end once I found the 'right person'. In the meantime I hung on to the demented rollercoaster that was my love life, telling myself, 'I'm going to stay in this relationship because he will become nicer/faithful/single.'

Learning about ADHD, and understanding that I was being driven by a motor with no clue where it was going, changed my life. I finally got off the rollercoaster. I have remained blissfully single for almost three years now and have taken time to step away, properly process things and heal. Healing from heartache is as vital as healing from any physical injury. These single years have been, and still are, one of the most incredible times of my life. The freedom I have is sweet joy. It's hard to explain how it feels without sounding like an inspirational quote on a gift-shop fridge magnet, but I've learned to treat myself with the utmost decency, compassion and care, and properly love myself. Though you'd think it would come naturally to not let into your life those who don't treat you in this way, for some of us it takes a long time to make sense of our own behaviour. I used to roll out the red carpet for all sorts of rapscallions, so long as they made me laugh and had pretty eyes.

In an interview, actor Emma Watson talked about being single and said she was 'self-partnered'. Understandably, it was taken by some to be a bit Paltrow/Martin/'consciously uncoupling' celebrity jargon, but boy, the woman hit the nail on the head. I cherish being 'self-partnered'. Properly single, not 'on the market' – just happily, deliciously single. Free to make every decision without checking in with anyone first. Free to give my time to whoever and whatever I please. Well-meaning people say, 'Oh, but you're amazing! How can you be single?', without knowing they might not have found the old me, ping-ponging from one agonising relationship to another, so 'amazing'. It's likely they wouldn't have formed any meaningful opinion of me at all . . . I'd have been glued to my phone having an intricate, time-consuming, utterly pointless texting row with someone who should only ever have been a fun one-night stand but now, inexplicably, had his own drawer in my house and my spare car keys. And they are fun these days – one-night stands – now that I want, at the very most, merely a warm friendship afterwards.

I invest far more meaningful time in friendships, now that my energy has been freed up. I've always taken great care to look after old friendships and have delighted in making new ones, too. The world is full of brilliant, kind and interesting people to get to know, and I have an incredible time indulging in connecting with more of them. I'm better at these relationships, and now I'm available to those I love in a way that I wasn't before.

As I get help with my ADHD, everything in my life is making more sense. My children have all of me, and that makes me happiest. The narrative of 'You have to have your own life, too' is one that is so often presented to me by people who don't understand that my children are my life. Childhood is short. I want to make the most of them before the day comes when I need to wait until they have a gap in their diary for me.

I speak regularly to my eighty-three-year-old Auntie Ashraf in Iran. When I talk with her, I feel no generation or cultural gap. She said to me, 'Cherish your freedom in not needing a partner. Now you know if you do have one again, it will only be because you have both truly fallen in love.'

For all my euphoria about falling in love with life on my own, I'm not ruling out a relationship in the future, but I'm not hoping, and I certainly am not looking for one. I know the more I work on myself, the less likely it will be that I fall back into the vortex of romantic chaos that I inhabited for so long. Mind and soul apart, I really enjoy not having the shoes of another person cluttering up my hallway again.

One Year Without Sex, Love or Dating

SHON FAYE

Being single throughout the first lockdown might not have been so hard if I hadn't begun 2020 still very much in a couple. I still remember the Christmas card he gave me and the message he wrote inside: 'I loved spending 2019 with you, looking forward to more in 2020 and beyond.' I so wanted that to be the case. But a month later we were both sat in the bedroom of his flat, faces red with tears and my case packed to leave for the last time. 'Can we still see each other?' he asked, his eyes glistening with the naïve hope of an adolescent. Yet his thirty-five-year-old rational brain must surely have told him the answer. He knew we couldn't. The reason for the split was as simple as it was life-shattering. He said he wanted children, one day. Children that I had never dreamed of myself, nor could ever give him, even if I wanted to.

They call it a deal breaker – the ultimate one really, as there is no hope and no compromise – yet the expression makes heartbreak sound like a boardroom negotiation. It would be more accurate to say the relationship had a terminal illness, and I chose to assist its death with dignity rather than let it carry on to an inevitable, but uglier, end years down the line. To me, it was a cataclysm that left me confounded by grief. Grief that felt more like physical pain for months. Months that, unfortunately, happened to coincide with a pandemic, which turned the other aspects of my life upside down, too.

'Now's the time to get really good at wanking,' my also recently single friend Gemma says matter-of-factly over WhatsApp voice-note, as if masturbation was a skill like kayaking or getting a soufflé to rise, before adding, 'and phone sex'. It was the end of March 2020 and the pressure was increasing on Boris Johnson to put the UK into a full lockdown. In the six weeks since my break-up, coronavirus had become a growing global disaster. The advice was clear: do not leave home, do not touch anyone, do not date, do not fuck.

Of course I could physically go without sex or dating – for the past six weeks I had done just that. But I also told everyone that this was 'actually fine'. Bragging constantly about a forthcoming summer of promiscuity was a lame attempt at a confidence trick on my own brain. In the immediate aftermath of my break-up, the idea of another man's touch or his weight on mine truly seemed inconceivable and undesirable. Yet when this became officially illegal, I panicked.

In the year after the start of the first lockdown, single people were largely ignored or erased in government communications about living with COVID restrictions. If, like me, you entered this pandemic single (or if you were in a couple where you don't cohabit), sex was technically illegal for a large portion of it. There was a brief period in 2020 when it was possible from July to October, but any new relationship embarked upon during that time would need to have become exclusive and cohabiting within a matter of weeks to have survived the second wave. It's safe to say that most of us who went into this pandemic single remained so, with little hope of change until the vaccine rollout kicked in during the summer of 2021.

Of course no one actually thought it would go on that long. Most of the official advice at the start wasn't dissimilar to my friend Gemma's – it was an era of Zoom dates, sex toys, phone sex and nudes, I was reassured by online magazines and sexual-health charities, all of which sounded very upbeat about this new era of remote sexuality. Even back then, I sensed they were missing the point. Sex and dating, for the newly single me, were about reprising an old ritual of encountering other people in order to rebuild a coherent picture of myself as a sexual being.

It's a common belief that any straight cis men who are titillated by the offer of sex with a transgender woman must be physically fetishising us. It's an analysis I've always found tedious and reductive of what even the most casual encounters with strangers have taught me about people and about life. Some years ago I anecdotally noticed that men on dating apps seemed much less bothered about the idea of being with a transsexual if they'd recently gone through a divorce or a long-term relationship had ended. Their once-imagined lives broken, they were hoping to see what a woman exiled from many heterosexual norms might have to teach them about their own failings. For years before I met my ex, I had gone 'for drinks' with the sort of man who secretly hopes that by tasting my deviance, he'll learn something more interesting about himself. It's a vampiric exchange; a contract of heat and blood. I suppose, after my relationship ended, I desperately hoped that the roles could be reversed. That post-break-up, with my own failed attempt at assimilating into heterosexuality, cis men might teach me about how to do normality better next time. That I would get to be the vampire.

Devoid of such luck, I instead spent significant parts of the first lockdown glued to Hinge and Tinder talking to people. In lieu of the ability to actually meet, I talked to men I might previously have swiftly turned down for a real date. I regaled my friends who were bored with lockdown with stories of my improbable virtual interactions. At one point that summer, for example, I was talking to three different Army officers (don't worry – different regiments!), despite the fact that my politics are anti-imperialist enough to question if soldiers should even exist. When Vera Lynn died in June 2020, my friend Huw cattily referred to me as 'our very own Forces' sweetheart' in the group chat.

At other times, the loneliness is too dark for jokes. Until things started to open up in July 2020 I was tormented by memories of my ex flooding back to me in the hours, days and weeks spent alone in lockdown. His hand on the small of my back on a crowded Tube platform; the time he rowed me around the Plaza de España in Seville and I took the piss the whole time, because being treated just like any other girl with a boyfriend on holiday was so unfamiliar;

the specific way the cadence of his breath would change during sex; the way his face would melt into a disarming smile when I'd outsmarted him in a debate about some political point or other.

One criticism of government policy during the pandemic is that it entrenched traditional norms in which only couples get the comfort of touch and intimacy. Having gone through the worst break-up of my life without even so much as a hug from a good friend or a gym class that promised to restore my self-worth, it is inevitable that there have been moments in the past two years when I regretted my decision to leave my relationship. In breaking up with him, I had taken the gamble to be single and make room for another life, more suited to my own long-term needs and desires. I hadn't chosen to be alone and bereft indefinitely.

Given the pandemic's side-effect of reinforcing socially conservative romantic arrangements and aspirations, my rejection of my ex's offer of precisely these things has also come back to haunt me at times. 'You're a transsexual and he was a tall, handsome, intelligent home-owner with great teeth: why the fuck did you do that?' my stimulus-starved brain started to bark at me. Sometimes the queries were crueller: 'Why don't you want to be a mother anyway?' the sadistic voice inside me asked. 'Not much of a woman after all, are you?'

Tired of second-guessing my own judgement, I've given up on the pursuit of dating seriously for now. It was brutal and I wouldn't wish it on anyone but, in the end, time did the work in healing me from my break-up – we have all lived with restrictions for so long that my relationship with my ex now feels like it took place in a different age. I can exchange a brief text with him now, or even visualise his future wife and kids, and not feel the searing pain. I can be glad he has the space for his own future, too.

It's not just time that's helped. A brief late-summer romance with a (slightly) younger man who unexpectedly slid into my DMs on Instagram managed to change my negative patterns of thinking about whether I'll be alone for ever; we didn't work out long-term, but dating him showed me it may work with someone else. A second break-up, even if less intense, followed by a second lockdown was a fucking chore. Again: no affirming spin class and no drinks with the girls. Since that whirlwind relationship ended so abruptly when we returned to lockdown in the autumn of 2020, the unsustainability of trying to build a serious relationship after all this solitude, anxiety and uncertainty has convinced me that I am not in a mindset to offer anyone else any kind of healthy relationship.

The pandemic has shown single and coupled people alike that all relationships are practical things, built more on a mixture of chance, timing, proximity and long-term compatibility than they are on initial chemistry or sexual desire, which you can have with many people. I loved my ex-boyfriend so much that, at times a few years ago, he seemed like my only true happiness. But it was still right that our relationship ended, as many have done during the pandemic for similar reasons: incompatibilities and insecurities were revealed, with the removal of distractions and overexposure to one another.

In the time since lockdowns began, I have relied so heavily on remote support from my friends that my yearning for romantic reassurance has receded, just as my need for in-person laughter and fun with my friends has grown to desperate levels. I long for the conviviality and spontaneity of the house party that runs until 6 a.m., the unplanned dinner out, the gossip and the sarcasm. After the hard work of surviving these lockdowns without friendship, how could the arduous work of building a lasting romantic love compete?

For years before I met the man I adored, then had to leave, I would imagine meeting someone like him and the life we would build together. I would daydream about how such a man would smooth over every scratch and dent left in my spirit by the unenviable tasks of being trans and a woman in this world, and make it stronger. Of course I hope I'll find love again after the pandemic, but I no longer fantasise about the more fulfilled and resilient and powerful woman I'll eventually turn into when I have it. Alone, I have already become her.

Why All Women Deserve to Experience Being Single in Their Thirties

SOPHIA LEONIE

On the day after I moved out of the home I shared with my partner of more than a decade, I went on a Tinder date. A London gastropub on a winter's work night. I couldn't even be bothered to change, and touched up my make-up in the work toilet before jumping on the Tube.

The date was, of course, disastrous. I thought it was a casual drink; he'd booked a table for a meal. The conversation was stilted and awkward. I was tired and heartbroken, which had manifested into sarcastic sharpness to a man who was simply trying to be complimentary. I made my excuses and disappeared into an Uber pretty quickly, to find that he'd messaged already: would I like to meet again? I blocked him.

But back home that night, as I snuggled into bed with my tea and episode of *Insecure*, I was proud of myself. Like my girl Issa, I did it. I had finally entered the scary, alien world of dating – and been liked. It didn't matter that it was awful; that I had no interest in him; that I made zero effort and left early. The point was I survived the unthinkable. Now, I knew that I could do this.

I was almost thirty-five and had unexpectedly found myself single. Single for the first time in my adult life. In the time that I had been coupled up, the UK had gone through four different prime ministers, smartphones had become the norm and social media had been invented. I had moved out of my family home, learned to drive, graduated from university and gained a PGCE, an MA and a career. I became a fully-fledged adult with my person by my side. We were intertwined in our journey into adulthood – and now I wasn't sure who I even was, or how to navigate the world without him.

Who would I call when something new and exciting happened? Who would I text to say I had got home safely? Who would I binge-watch that new series with? Who would I go shopping for? These thoughts would rise at unexpected moments and cause me an ongoing, crippling anxiety. There was one recurring thought in particular that caused me the most anxiety. One thought that, no matter how much I tried to rationalise, refused to go away: I had reached my mid-thirties with no man, no marriage and no kids – and now it was all too late.

In reality, I wasn't late for anything. The Office for National Statistics (ONS) reported in 2017 that the average age at which straight couples marry is thirty-five for women and thirty-eight for men. Yet I had an overwhelming feeling of failure and shame about my new situation. This both surprised and disappointed me. I had never even wanted to get married. To me, it was a trap to distract girls from aspiring to achievements outside the home, one that ensured a woman's identity stayed tied to a man's. I had never wanted children – they would take away my freedom, change my body and derail my career. It was just another exhausting expectation that I pushed back against. So why did I feel like such a failure?

Online, it suddenly seemed that these traditional expectations were being embraced by everyone my age and younger. And honestly – it all looked great. Romance was everywhere: the *Love Island* couple, the ex-popstar duo or even that friend who has gone Insta-official with their new beau. It's hard not to get sucked in. Their love story is our entertainment, escapism, even . . . inspiration. But we forget that it's also a construction. A carefully plotted narrative designed to make us insecure and envious.

A survey reported by Yahoo in 2019 found that of 2,800 couples, 42 per cent feel pressure to ensure their wedding is Instagrammable. Yes – people are literally designing their big days with us, the largely anonymous scrollers of the apps, in mind. And this applies not just to weddings, but also to the portrayal of relationships in general online. Half (51 per cent) of millennials show their relationship as happier than it really is, and 42 per cent use social media to give the impression of a 'perfect relationship', according to a study by the relationship support charity Relate. Of course, when at your most insecure, it's almost impossible to rationalise what you're seeing. Especially when your algorithm keeps giving you more of the poison – leading you further down the rabbit hole.

These images became beyond exhausting. And despite my own positive, put-together profile, I couldn't bear the thought of performing for the patriarchy a moment longer. One day I pressed that little X on the app icon and deleted my account.

Whilst I knew my poorly timed, premature date was not trying to actually find a mate for marriage, I also knew the idea of moving on with my life was still rooted in being chosen by a partner, and being desired. And yes – that feels really good, especially if you've recently been taken for granted. But I was tired of my own idea of self-worth being defined by my ability to give a man a hard-on and sustain his interest.

Like many of us, I learned before I entered my teens that my function as a female was to be attractive to men. Immediately after I began to develop, aged twelve, boys – and, more often, adult men – would harass me in public: coming home from school; on the bus; shopping. By my mid-teens I learned that this attention was a test. You failed if you seemed too keen (that is, you were 'easy' and unsuitable for 'wifeying'). You failed if you were too 'stush' (that is, you dared to reject and thus emasculate them). Even as I entered my twenties and my confidence to navigate these situations grew, the power imbalance remained the same. This was the late 1990s and early 2000s: a time before 'feminist' was a T-shirt slogan, before 'consent' was a buzzword, or 'MeToo' a hashtag. Before dating apps enabled you to narrow down the type of man you actually wanted, actively vetting their interests, values and goals. Back then, it was accepted that you were passive in the courting process. Club Colosseum wasn't quite the Debutantes' Ball – but we knew, whilst donning our best designer jeans, chainmail boob-tube and shimmer lipstick, that we'd be 'chirpsed' and would make our choice from the narrow selection of numbers stored in our waiting Nokias.

Maybe that was why I felt like a failure in my thirties, post-break-up. I'd internalised the pressure to be the right kind of girl, so I'd meet the right guy who chooses, and thus validates, me. Perhaps my fierce opposition to marriage and kids was a façade. Certainly most women I knew in their thirties had ended up conforming to social expectations – married, or with children. New in my singledom, I envied them so bad it hurt. But as I got used to being single, something slowly changed. From the periphery, the women of my generation – particularly ones who had entered into their relationships at a young age – looked stuck. Stuck in mundane routine; stuck in a job they hated, but needed; stuck with an inadequate man, but lacking the confidence or finances to leave. And here I was, completely free, with the unexpected opportunity to re-evaluate my life. So, with nothing to lose, I did exactly that.

First, I knew I needed a new work–life balance. Sure, I had a career – but not in what I really wanted and it was increasingly making me unhappy. I took the plunge and negotiated one day off a week, knowing the dip in income would be just about manageable and I could use that day to work on what I really loved: writing. This got me my first-ever commission and was the beginning of an exciting, fulfilling new career.

Second, I needed to expand my friendship circle: meet new people – women like myself who were actively trying not to define themselves through their relationship with men. Whilst social media had been unhelpful initially, I discovered that, when used correctly, you could connect with interesting, like-minded people. Upon return from my digital detox, I un-followed anyone who made me feel insecure, only following accounts that inspired me. I forged new and very real friendships that transcended into IRL.

During my two years of being single in my mid-thirties I did things I never would have done had I been in a relationship – simply because I was able to consider for the first time who I was; what I wanted; and how I was going to achieve it without considering how someone else fitted into that. I felt fulfilled, confident and therefore more open to taking risks. I flat-shared with a friend in the centre of town, I went regularly out on week nights, I saw an abundance of theatre and art, dated again, wrote poetry, articles and a play, and I travelled.

Walking down Venice Beach one evening during a three-month solo trip to LA, I'll never forget the huge sense of euphoria I felt, knowing the whole world was out there – and I was finding the bits I liked, constructing a life that would truly make me happy.

It's not that when we're in a long-term relationship we actively decide not to take risks, not to meet new people or not to travel to another country alone – we just generally . . . don't. There's a false sense of safety and security in a relationship. And make no mistake: love is great, and all women deserve to experience that. But it's time to shift the narrative: all women deserve to experience being single in their thirties, too.

Because despite what Instagram might tell you, you're not too late for anything; there are many ways to live your life. We don't exist to be chosen or desired by some man – it's a myth that we grew up with, de-centring us from being the protagonists of our own lives.

Empowering, Not Embarrassing: Why Egg-Freezing Shouldn't Feel Shameful

SOPHIA MONEY-COUTTS

I first came across the shame that surrounds egg-freezing when my friend Ali asked if I'd drive her to hospital before her egg-retrieval operation (also known as the day your eggs are 'collected' or 'harvested'; fertility terminology often sounds like it's plucked from *The Handmaid's Tale*). Ali had told very few people that she was going through freezing because she was embarrassed about it, and since I had a car, she asked me. I said yes, course, and one morning in November 2018 I chauffeured her to hospital.

Once there, we checked in (I'm pretty sure all the staff thought we were an item) and were shown to a hospital room, where Ali changed into her backless operation gown and I ate a Pret baguette. This was particularly unsupportive nursing on my part, since she wasn't allowed to eat anything before her general anaesthetic.

Not long afterwards she was taken down to theatre for a twenty-minute procedure, where a doctor pushed a thin metal needle through her vaginal wall to collect the eggs she'd been growing, with the help of hormone injections, for the previous few weeks. When she was wheeled back from her operation, we both cried: Ali because she'd been through a physical and emotional ordeal; I because I was proud of her for making this choice, and sad that she felt she needed to keep it a secret. Also because my boyfriend and

I had recently separated and he'd moved out. I was thirty-three, single again, so maybe now I had to consider egg-freezing, too?

It took more than a year to decide that it was the right call for me, during which time I went to an egg-freezing open evening at a different London hospital. Plenty of fertility clinics offer these free talks, so I figured it would be worth going along and seeing if it helped me make up my mind. Plus, the website mentioned complimentary coffee and biscuits.

I came across the same shame here, too. Each time another woman came through the door, I'd look up from the statistics and we'd make a small, nervous smile at one another before she headed towards the back of the room.

These were professional women in their thirties with nice hair, handbags I'd seen in magazines and work clothes which suggested they had their professional shit together. But it felt like there was a cloak of embarrassment hanging over the room. Coming to this talk, and even thinking about undergoing egg-freezing, was the dream of nobody here when they were younger and trying to imagine their future life. And yet we were single, and headlines in the *Daily Mail* had started to make us panic about our ovaries, so we were about to spend our Tuesday evening watch a doctor run a laser pen over a succession of alarming graphs.

That was the evening I decided in favour of egg-freezing. The doctor was convincing, and I was a good age for the success rates to be high enough (at thirty-five, if you freeze the recommended number of twenty eggs, this gives you 70–90 per cent chance of a baby later on). It was also the evening I resolved to record the process and make a podcast about it, because the shame and embarrassment the women in that room so obviously felt about confronting their fertility seemed medieval.

Look, egg-freezing is no picnic. One round takes about a month, and I spent that month watching my emotions roll up and down like a small child's. Tears one minute; a surprising bounciness the next. For the first two weeks I inhaled a nasal spray, which stopped my brain talking to my reproductive system, in order to prevent any eggs being released too early. For the second two weeks

I also injected the roll of fat beneath my belly button with a short, stubby needle every night, encouraging more eggs to grow. One Sunday evening I cried because the needle wouldn't slide in and it felt so pathetic, doing this by myself in my bedroom. I also had to give up coffee, blew up like a water balloon and it cost me nearly £5,000.

But at the end of that month I got twenty-two eggs, which are now sitting in a cold, squat tank that looks like something from a sci-fi film. They're no guarantee of a baby, but should provide a pretty good shot if I need them in the future. To me, this feels empowering, not embarrassing, because it's given me more choice at a stage when it can feel, for women, as if our options are narrowing with every month that passes.

I understand the shame completely. If you're considering freezing, it will force you to confront certain questions. Some of these are practical: can I afford it? Aren't the success rates said to be woeful? Will the synthetic hormones make me feel deranged? (Quite possibly.) Some of the questions are bigger and more philosophical, and they may underline a wistful sense of failure that you may feel about life not having worked out like you imagined. As I slid through my thirties, why did it feel as if all my friends were so many steps ahead of me in life? Was I being too picky when it came to men, hoping for the unattainable? Did I even want children?

Choosing to freeze your eggs can therefore feel like you've got life wrong when everybody else seems to have got it right. But the truth is, on a planet of more than seven billion people, not everyone will do things at the same time, and egg-freezing may give you more flexibility – some breathing space – instead of panicking about finding the single guy at every social event you go to. Trust me, I have been there. I have attended friends' weddings and cased the marquee like a hungry piranha and it did not make me feel good about myself. What made me feel good about myself was choosing to freeze my eggs rather than give in to the relentless societal pressure to meet someone. Life is not over if you haven't got a husband, a Le Creuset casserole dish and a baby by the time you're thirty-five.

The morning after my operation, even though I'd spent months researching freezing and interviewing women who'd gone through it, I was startled by the sense of relief. Again I want to reiterate that my eggs are no guarantee of a baby down the line and, for *Freezing Time*, my podcast series, I spoke to two women who froze their eggs and, sadly, failed to have children with them. But I still felt as if I'd clawed back some time. Who knows, a handsome stranger who understands the importance of dental floss may appear in my life tomorrow and I may never need those eggs. But if not, then I have options, and anything that gives women more choice and independence is very much endorsed by me.

I don't want to sound like I'm pushing freezing on anyone. It's a very personal choice. But if you do decide in favour of it, please try and find some pride in knowing that you've made a difficult decision and are doing something for you, rather than capitulating to a timeline that society, and potentially your parents or grandparents, believe you should be following instead.

Not long before I started my round of freezing, I went to a dinner thrown by a family friend. A woman in her sixties who I didn't know struck up a conversation with me, using the following line: 'Hello, what's going on in your life? Have you got a nice man?' I smiled and waved one hand towards my vagina. 'No, actually, I'm about to have my eggs frozen,' which made her turn rather pale. But this cannot be the first question that women 'of a certain age' are asked today. No, thank you. Not any more.

Egg-freezing isn't perfect, or an insurance policy, and it costs a dizzying sum of money, but it gives some women more liberty at an age when it feels like we come to a fork in the road and have to make the decision there and then: baby or no baby? This is why some fertility experts have labelled it 'the second wave of emancipation, after the invention of the pill'. I'll take that.

The Journey of Being Plus-Size and Single

STEPHANIE YEBOAH

'I'm sorry, Steph. It's just . . . you don't have the right kind of shape I like; I like hourglass plus-size women.'

It was February 2017 and I was in bed staring up at the ceiling, trying to hold back tears as my ex-boyfriend cited the reasons he had decided to break up with me at 12.30 a.m. At twenty-seven years old, this had been my first and only relationship, and as my ex continued to use my fat body as the reason he no longer wanted to continue being with me, all I could think of was, 'I've failed at my one and only shot at being happy; maybe I've always been destined to be single.'

shrugs

Let's start at the beginning.

Act I

As it stands now, being single has become a way of life for me – I literally know no other way in which to exist otherwise. I knew from a very young age that I would probably always be alone, as I always knew that the shape of my body would hinder any chances I would have of finding love or genuine intimacy. I know it may sound presumptuous to go straight for my appearance as being the sole reason, but I'm very confident in my personality (I've won 'best personality' thrice at Speed Dating events, don't ya know) and would be super-aware if my singledom was due to anything outside of how I looked.

While all the girls in secondary school were having their first kisses, cheeky gropes in deserted classrooms and daily lunchtime group meetings about the several hours spent talking to their crushes on the phone the previous night, I was drifting aimlessly through school on my own in my uniform that consisted of super-baggy grunge jeans and an oversized hoodie; invisible and yet hyper-visible at the same time, due to my size.

I experienced physical and verbal abuse throughout school, due to being fat. Because of this, it made me unapproachable to others, thus causing me to have few-to-no friends as a teenager. Having gone through several eating disorders and self-harm practices in a bid to shed my fat and feel better in myself, I came to the conclusion that I would always be single and blamed my body for this; thus triggering the start of an almost fifteen-year war with my body.

As unfortunate as it is, desirability politics and body privilege will also be a deciding factor when it comes to dating and relationships. As someone who resides in a darker-skinned, fat body, I always knew that the way I looked wouldn't be considered as aesthetically pleasing in accordance with the Westernised standards of beauty. Thus I drifted through life feeling unworthy of love or desire. My body carries traits that would be seen as the direct antithesis of what constitutes femininity: fatter bodies within society are seen as unfeminine, grotesque and subhuman. Black women have historically been given tropes such as 'angry', 'difficult', 'aggressive' and 'fiery', and our beauty has always been seen as inferior or relevant for the purposes of hypersexuality. When you add being a darker-skinned woman on top of that? Whew! The colourism racks up the undesirability aspect astronomically, due to darker skin being seen as dirty, masculine, unintelligent and ugly.

I grew older and I internalised these negative feelings, watching my peers fall in love, date, lose their virginity and settle down, while I continued on the path of doing everything within my body to make myself more palatable. I tried bleaching my skin, which proved unsuccessful, as my skin didn't take to the harmful chemicals. I tried fasting and going on extreme diets, in a bid to force an hourglass shape out of me. I tried going out with my girlfriends to bars, days out, restaurants and events, only to end up as the single invisible amongst the group at the end of the night.

So of course it was a shock to me when I ended up in my first relationship (which also housed my first kiss and first ... well everything) at the age of twenty-five and it was – to all intents and purposes – an OK relationship, for the most part. I was in a relationship where I felt appreciated, loved and desired (or so I thought at the time). I was absolutely *sick* in love and thought that this guy – this conventionally attractive, super-handsome man who was the exact aesthetic opposite of me in every way – would be the one I would grow old with! We'd get married! And move to Oxford, somewhere on a farm! Kids and pets galore! This would come crashing down a couple of years later, as my weight became his sole reason for breaking up with me. In that moment everything spiralled, and so began 2017, my *annus horribilis*.

Act II

This was also the year that, while incredibly heartbreaking and depressing, ultimately changed not only how I viewed my self-worth and my body, but also how I viewed being a single woman at an age when everyone around me seemed to be making moves with their 'baes' to buy property and start families.

The break-up was in March 2017; however, we did what I like to call the annoying 'back-and-forth break-up tango that lasted six and a half months'. This mostly consisted of virtual silence for three months, followed by another three months of 'I think we could be platonic friends, let's meet up!' conversations, which led to another three weeks of suppressed emotions, mixed feelings, declarations of lingering love (from my side), false re-couplings and closure chats, only to end with another woman sending me an email in the middle of night about her trysts with my ex while we were together. *Lovely!*

Ultimately, our last conversation ended with him telling me that he preferred 'hourglass-shaped' women, and that my body wasn't the body type he preferred. As someone who has been on a lifelong journey with learning how to love my fat body, this declaration managed to break me completely. My confidence and self-esteem evaporated into the ether.

Moving back to my parents' home and losing my job directly after the break-up only served to push my state of mind into further decline. I was lonely, depressed, suicidal and I felt like a failure. Once again I blamed my body for the circumstances I found myself in. I cried every day for a year straight, praying to God that my ex would one day find it in his heart to take me back. I felt pathetic, to tell you the truth, and much as I tried to initiate a 'whore phase' to numb the pain, my body type meant that I was unsuccessful in even trying to get men to sleep with me.

Singledom, to me, felt like a birthright. Something I was destined to carry for the rest of my life, due to the way I looked. One day I reached a point when I realised that crying wasn't going to bring my ex back. I realised that pining over men who I thought were unattainable wasn't going to make me feel any more valuable. An epiphany occurred in early 2018, and I realised that I could not allow the shallow, narrow-minded actions of a man to make me feel less than the amazing person I was.

I slowly began to climb out of the depths of my depression and loneliness and started blogging again, as well as getting therapy, which helped immensely. I deleted the dating apps and concentrated on going out with my friends more. I learned how to improve my make-up and hairstyling skills. I tried to fill my days with things that didn't revolve around needing a partner. I started treating myself: buying beautiful pieces of lingerie that made me feel spectacular, and I would walk around my flat wearing nothing but those pieces. Man, was it empowering!

The year of 2018 was one of reinvention, and I tried as much as possible to get my groove back. One of the things I realised in that year was how complacent I had become while I was in that relationship. I had a man, and that was the beginning and end of my story, so why would I need to have any more goals? Although I was blogging intensively at the time, with my profile starting to rise, I was perfectly happy settling for being in a minimum-wage job and not making any effort, because I had a *man*!

But Steph *sans* man? She had more time to concentrate on her blog and writing. She had more time to network with peers, discover new career opportunities, fine-tune her skills and, ultimately, forge a career as a multi-award-winning content creator and journalist. Had I not been single, I wouldn't have had the motivation and tenacity to turn my career around and transform into the person I am today.

I am at a place in my life now where I still sometimes feel bouts of sadness about being chronically single. There is a lot I still haven't experienced when it comes to intimacy, love, desire and companionship, and these are all things that one day I desperately hope to have. But with it come feelings of completeness; it comes with knowing my worth, and not settling for someone who always saw me as something to do 'in the meantime'.

Being single has taught me that I have a host of amazing qualities that I probably would never have discovered in myself, had I stayed in that relationship. It's taught me how to love my body separately from the approval of others. It's taught me that I absolutely *love* my own company. It's taught me that my body is something worthy of desire, love, respect and the basic human decency that everyone should be afforded. It's taught me that I can still want and be on the lookout for romantic love, and doing so doesn't mean that I don't love myself.

I managed to turn what was my worst-case scenario into something beautiful for myself. I lost the man, but I gained so much more in return. I gained the ability to love myself loudly and without shame; and, most importantly, I learned that never again will I sit and hope for someone to choose me; I'm the one who gets to do the choosing and, when I do, that person will love all of me – stretch marks, cellulite, FUPA and all – proudly and unapologetically.

Me, Myself and My Toys

VENUS LIBIDO

When I was a teen, being overly interested in sex or having a lot of sex gave you a name that you didn't want to be stuck with at that age. On the other hand, if you weren't having sex, you were considered frigid, uninteresting and prudish. It was a real double-edged sword that would confuse any young, sexually curious teen. On top of that, having very minimal sex education, conversations around sexuality, self-pleasure and consent was the cherry on top of the cake.

Up until the age of twenty-one I considered sex to be something you just did rather than something you enjoyed – the thought of communicating what I did enjoy, or where I liked to be touched during sex, never crossed my mind. I never saw other women communicating what they wanted pre- and during sex in films or even in porn, so I assumed men knew what they were doing and that what they did do had a happy ending for both parties.

Despite all the above, the biggest obstacle I faced, growing up, was that I felt a strong sexual attraction towards other women. However, being attracted to the same sex was not something people admitted when I was younger, even though the first three people I ever kissed were girls. I was always sworn to secrecy not to spill the beans. Being gay was considered funny and a joke when I was a teen, so out of fear of bullying, nothing was ever said or admitted to my peers or, at times, to myself.

I remember very clearly, around the age of thirteen, hanging out at a boy's house one day after school with a friend. He thought it would be funny if we all watched lesbian porn together, which would be the first time I'd ever seen porn. He was a little older than us, so we said yes, thinking it was the cool thing to do. The whole time they both laughed and made homophobic jokes that made me uncomfortable, and I remember feeling sick to my stomach. I couldn't admit it, but I enjoyed watching two women have sex with each other, and I felt very turned on and curious at the time.

I knew from a very young age that I was attracted to women; while I'm opening up about my gay fantasies, my first true love was Disney's animated character Kim Possible, and then, later on, Raven-Symoné from *That's So Raven*. I remember desperately wanting to watch and explore more lesbian porn after that afternoon. However, accessing porn when I was a teen involved a deafening dial-up tone in a house where we only had one computer. In other words, privacy was a no-no and watching porn was an even bigger no-no, so I had to get creative with my thoughts.

Outside of school, I was surrounded by different forms of relationships and sexual orientations. My mum played for an all-female ice-hockey team where the majority of the women identified as lesbian or bisexual and gender-fluid. I spent most weekends on coaches travelling with them to away-games and in locker rooms, where I would watch women feel comfortable with their bodies and sexuality in an open and positive environment. To this day, I still look back and remember how at home I felt being around them and looking forward to the weekends away with these women, who I looked up to so much.

As you can imagine, I was at a real crossroads when it came to my sexuality. If I decided to come out, I wasn't sure if my parents would be angry and reject me as their child. If my friends found out, would they all laugh at me and bully me? Would I have to move school? I felt a real sense of rejection everywhere I looked. So, out of fear, I conformed to what was expected of me and suppressed everything else.

Most of my intimate relationships while growing up – and there weren't many – were with men who, if I'm frank with myself, I didn't want to be with. The ones I did have a relationship with were long-term. I always stayed longer than I should have, which I now know is mainly linked to some childhood trauma. I couldn't face people coming and going out of my life, so any attachment that I had with someone, including friends, was hard to let go of, even when it was an unhealthy relationship.

I remained a closeted pansexual right up until the age of twenty-nine, expressing my sexuality only in the girls' toilets on nights out, just like when I was a teen. When it came to expressing my sexuality and interests, I was always private and never open. The only person who was privy to my desires was my male best friend, who also identifies as gay. I saw him as the only person I knew would understand.

To this day, I don't fully feel like my whole self when it comes to my identity, and that's something I'm still working on. However, a considerable transformation came at the start of 2020, shortly after turning twenty-nine. It was coming up to my tenth anniversary with my then boyfriend. He knew I was pansexual, as I'd come out to him a few years before. He was comfortable with it, but wasn't comfortable exploring that part of me together. For many years I felt unfulfilled, especially towards the end of the relationship. So at the start of 2020, two weeks into the new year, I knew I had to end it. New year, new me, and all that. I remember waking up that day and thinking, 'I can't continue being in a relationship where I'm lying to myself about what I want and who I am.' I was heartbroken, and to this day I regard it as the most challenging thing I've ever done in my life. Not only because I find it hard to let people go – and this person knew me inside out – but also because I was finally coming out and not hiding a part of me that I'd kept concealed for so long. I had no idea how my family would react.

Later that week I sat down with my mum and told her everything. In truth, I had nothing to worry about, and I'm fortunate to have a family which accepts that part of me. I am now a very out and proud pansexual, who loves to talk about sex and isn't afraid to look at my vagina. I have a wall shrine of sex toys and get paid to bare all on the internet. I've come a long way.

A question I am asked a lot is what made me confident about discussing sex, dating, relationships and masturbation now? Well, rewind to 2019. I had an excellent idea for a TV show. I hadn't seen many people giving the LGBTQI+ community a chance to talk about their sex lives, dating and relationships in an educational, fun and informative way. So I thought, 'Why not me?' It would allow me to dive into a topic that I felt I had to shy away from for many years, and potentially answer many questions I had about myself. Sex was something I couldn't stop thinking about, and from a young age I had been sexually curious. I always wanted to talk about it, I developed an obsession with exploring my sexuality and I wanted to surround myself with sexually confident out-and-proud humans to help me on my way.

The show picked up a big sponsor by a sex-toy brand that loved the idea, and ended up being a success. I formed relationships with people who made me re-evaluate who I was and what I wanted. Since then I've delved further into the topic of sex and self-exploration, which is a journey that remains endless and ever-evolving, ultimately leading to the big break-up.

Since then I've thrown myself at opportunities that push me out of my comfort zone, which I never did when I was in a relationship. Looking back, I leaned on my other half way too much. I have pushed myself to be vulnerable, to never feel shame or guilt again, and I most certainly never hide anything about myself when I enter new relationships. Most of all, I gave myself the break I needed to figure things out. To figure *me* out.

Sex has always been the answer for me – sex with myself, to be precise. There was always something missing for me when it came to sex with other people. It was good, don't get me wrong, but I was doing it all wrong. I wasn't selfish, and I wasn't in tune with myself and my body, which in turn only left me feeling unsatisfied. I genuinely believe now that having sex with myself regularly has changed my whole perspective, not just on what I want, but what I see when I look at myself. Sex with other people is not a guessing game any more, and I most certainly don't assume that the other person knows how my body works. A massive benefit of masturbating is that it improves self-esteem and body image. When you start to love your whole body – genitals included – extraordinary things can happen, your mindset will change and your body will feel a new lease of life.

Having sex with myself has opened a door where I try to let

myself go on the other side. Every experience is different, and the more I do it, the more I learn about myself. For example, I never treated myself to lingerie because I thought it was a waste of money. I always told myself it wasn't worth it, as it only ends up on the floor anyway. However, when I stopped thinking about other people and started focusing on myself, I realised I did want lingerie, and I loved looking at myself in the mirror when wearing it. I began to look at myself as sexy, and I started to enjoy my own company. Now I can spend hours just looking, touching and feeling myself, with no awkwardness or shame afterwards.

After the show went live, I had floods of emails from companies that wanted me to try their sex toys. One toy review led to another, and now I have more than sixty toys in my collection. I currently review at least one toy a month on my socials, and another two in my newsletter. My room is a shrine of sex toys, and I love it!

Many people view sex toys as a replacement for sex, but they are an enhancement and can do things the human body can't. One toy will give me sensations that another cannot, and that's what's so intriguing about them. Toys can also help those who have medical conditions. As someone who lives with endometriosis, I can find penetrative sex painful at times. I do a lot of research on toys and products that can help with pain, especially toys that can help make sex with a partner more comfortable and enjoyable. The best part of what I do, and what I enjoy the most, is supporting other women who think their sex lives need to end because they experience pain during penetrative sex. I refuse to let that happen, because I've seen how much pleasure and self-love have helped me and, at times, saved me.

I think it's important to remind yourself of the benefits of masturbation because, for many people, the topic makes them uncomfortable, but it's something we can all benefit from. I was once one of them – don't worry. But something that I remind myself and others who find the conversation uncomfortable is that sex, with or without a partner, is just as natural as eating, sleeping and breathing. Now I encourage you to explore your body, dig out those dusty toys, move those fingers down south and allow yourself to feel a rush that you so rightly deserve.

References

Ketaki Chowkhani

Sri Aurobindo. *Savitri*
Sri Aurobindo. *Letters on Himself and the Ashram*
Sri Aurobindo. *Collected Poems*
The Mother. *Some Answers from the Mother*
The Mother. *Words of the Mother II*
Michael Cobb. *Single: Arguments for the Uncoupled*
Bella DePaulo. *How We Live Now: Redefining Home and Family in the 21st Century*
Elyakim Kislev. *Happy Singlehood: The Rising Acceptance and Celebration of Solo Living*
Eric Klinenberg. *Going Solo: The Extraordinary Rise and Surprising Appeal of Living Alone*
Kinneret Lahad. *A Table for One: A Critical Reading of Singlehood, Gender and Time*
Craig Wynne. *How to Be a Happy Bachelor*
https://www.chronicle.com/article/make-room-for-singles-in-teaching-and-research/
https://www.thehindubusinessline.com/blink/know/table-for-one-please/article31050738.ece
https://www.psychologytoday.com/us/blog/living-single/201103/solitude-part-2-the-benefits-it-brings-and-the-special-strengths-the
https://www.psychologytoday.com/us/blog/living-single/201503/finding-the-one-is-overrated-emotionships-matter-more
https://www.youtube.com/watch?v=8sdJAXIQ9T4

About the Editor

ANGELICA MALIN is an award-winning entrepreneur based in London. She is the founder and Editor-in-Chief of *About Time Magazine*, one of the UK's leading lifestyle magazines, and runs #SheStartedItLIVE, a festival of female empowerment. Angelica is also the author of *She Made It: The Toolkit for Female Founders in the Digital Age*.

About the Contributors

ANNIE LORD grew up in Otley, a town on the outskirts of Leeds. While attending Newcastle University she had a column on sex and relationships in the university paper. After graduating she began writing for a number of publications, including *VICE*, *The Sunday Times*, *New Statesman*, *The Independent* and more. She now has a dating column in *Vogue*. Her first book, *Notes on Heartbreak*, is published in 2022.

ASHLEY JAMES is a presenter and DJ, and has also become an inspirational figure on social media. Although she is now a new mum, Ashley spent six years of her life single. During this time, Ashley transformed her mindset to live a life of single positivity and even trained as an empowerment coach to help others feel the same. By using her coaching accreditation and influence, Ashley uses her social media presence to empower women on a range of topics from motherhood to dating. Known for her refreshingly honest and authentic social commentary, Ashley has become known as a trusted voice in the digital world and has collaborated with many well-known brands. Ashley is also a familiar face on British Television and has worked hard to forge a reputation of professionalism, relatability and great entertainment.

BELLA DEPAULO (PhD, Harvard) has always been single and always will be. *The Atlantic* magazine calls her 'America's foremost thinker and writer on the single experience'. She has bylines in *The New York Times*, *The Washington Post*, *New York* magazine, *The Atlantic*, *Time* magazine, *The Guardian*, *The Chronicle* *of Higher Education*, NBC, CNN and many more. She is the author of *Singled Out: How Singles Are Stereotyped, Stigmatized, and Ignored, and Still Lives Happily Ever After* and other books, and has been writing the 'Living Single' blog for *Psychology Today* since 2008. Her TEDx Talk, 'What no one ever told you about people who are single', has been viewed more than a million times.

CHANTÉ JOSEPH is a freelance writer, digital-content producer and host of Channel 4's *How Not To Be Racist* and *The Face* magazine's *My Public Me* podcast. She frequently writes for platforms including British *Vogue*, *Complex*, *The Guardian*, the *i* newspaper, *The Huffington Post*, *VICE*, *gal-dem*, Soho House and more. In 2018 she wrote her first-ever cover story for *Wonderland* magazine, interviewing Beyoncé's very own Chloe and Halle. She has recently hosted live streams for TikTok and collaborated with brands such as Bumble, Adidas, Spotify and YouTube. Chanté has also written her first book, *A Quick Ting On: The Black British Power Movement*, published in 2021.

CHARLIE CRAGGS is an award-winning trans activist, author and media personality, dubbed 'the voice of a community' by *Vogue*, best known for her campaign 'Nail Transphobia', her Lambda-nominated book *To My Trans Sisters* and her BBC documentary *Transitioning Teens*. Since 2013 she has been offering the public free manicures for the chance to sit down and have a chat with a trans person, in a bid to break misconceptions and make allies. In 2016 Charlie topped *The Guardian*'s New Radicals list of social innovators in Britain and has gone on to speak at the Houses of Parliament, win a *Marie Claire* Future Shapers Award and front global campaigns for brands such as the Body Shop, H&M and Selfridges.

CHLOE PIERRE is a digital marketer and a content creator, working with the likes of H&M, Monki, Pinterest, Nike, Jordan, Samsung, M&S and Calvin Klein. She is the founder of the wellness community thy.self, which aims to actualise self-care online

About the Contributors

and in real life as well as diversify the wellness community, both within the UK and internationally.

FELICITY MORSE is an author, former journalist and confidence coach. She works to help support people in connecting with their most capable creative selves and in setting up a life that is an expression of that.

FRANCESCA SPECTER is a London-based journalist, podcaster and the founder of Alonement – a platform dedicated to exploring alone-time and why it matters. Formerly Deputy Lifestyle Editor at Yahoo, Francesca has worked for the *Daily Express*, *Healthy* magazine and British *Vogue* and has written on a freelance basis for *The Telegraph*, *The Independent* and *Red*. She has an MA in Magazine Journalism from City University. She started the 'Alonement' blog in 2019, and launched her podcast of the same name in early 2020 – interviewing guests including Alain de Botton, Poorna Bell and Daisy Buchanan. Her first book, *Alonement*, empowers readers to value their own company and dedicate quality time to themselves, whoever they are and whatever their relationship status.

JESSICA MORGAN is a British NCTJ-accredited journalist, writer, editor, broadcaster, speaker and brand consultant based in Essex. She is currently Refinery29 UK's staff writer and heads up R29 Unbothered UK. She covers breaking news, current affairs, women's issues, sustainability, entertainment, beauty, fashion and lifestyle stories. Her freelance work has been featured in *The Times*, *Grazia*, *Elle*, *Refinery29* UK, *Harper's Bazaar*, *The Independent*, *Evening Standard*, Black Ballad, *gal-dem*, Soho House, *TimeOut London*, *Stylist* and *Red* magazine. In 2020 Jessica was shortlisted for New Journalist of the Year at the British Journalism Awards. She also won second place in *VICE*'s EMEA Impact Award.

KETAKI CHOWKHANI works in the faculty of sociology at the Manipal Centre for Humanities, Manipal Academy of Higher

Education, India. She researches and teaches singles studies and gender studies. She has a PhD in Women's Studies from the Tata Institute of Social Sciences, Mumbai. Her doctoral work focused on sexuality education and adolescent masculinities in middle-class Mumbai. Her writing has appeared in the *Indian Journal of Medical Ethics*, *Journal of Porn Studies*, *The New York Times*, *In Plainspeak*, *Teacher Plus*, *DNA*, Kafila.online, Round Table India and *Ultraviolet*. Ketaki also has an MPhil in Cultural Studies from the English and Foreign Languages University and an MA in English from Pondicherry University.

LUCIE BROWNLEE is a multi-award-winning writer based in County Durham, with her daughter and two dogs. Her memoir, *Life After You*, was published in 2014 by Penguin Random House. Based on her award-winning blog 'Wife After Death' (Blog North Awards 2013), the memoir is described by Richard Madeley as 'warm, moving, and often extremely funny'. It is a *Sunday Times* bestseller and was a Richard and Judy Autumn Book Club pick in 2015. Lucie's TV pilot, *Wife After Death*, was named Best New Comedy Script in the All3Media New Voice Awards 2021 and is currently in development with Objective Media.

MADELEINE SPENCER is an award-winning journalist, podcaster, broadcaster and make-up artist who has written for titles including *InStyle UK*, *Marie Claire*, *Elle UK*, *Porter*, *Glamour UK*, *Metro*, *The Huffington Post* and *Stylist*. Her podcast, *Beauty Full Lives*, is an interview series and has featured in the top-fifty podcasts chart on iTunes, as well as in *Get the Gloss*, *Marie Claire*, *Elle UK*, *Harper's Bazaar*, the *Daily Mail*, *Hello!*, *Arcadia* and *You* magazine. Madeleine's blog, on MadeleineLoves.com, covers product reviews, travel, mental health and features some of her work as a journalist and make-up artist. She has also offered commentary on *Newsnight*, ITV, Sky News and various BBC radio stations and writes about mental health, travel (with a focus on retreats and wellness holidays) and life's little niggles.

About the Contributors

MEGAN BARTON-HANSON is an English media personality, columnist and host of the chart-topping podcast *You Come First*. She is best known for her appearance in the 2018 series of the hit reality show *Love Island*. After leaving the villa as one of the most sought-after TV personalities, Megan has since built an unapologetic and successful business helping women to liberate themselves through body positivity and freedom of sexuality. She has used her courageous and candid approach regarding her own life experiences to give young women an honest, supportive and safe space, as well as the confidence to share their own stories regarding their sexuality, physical and mental-health issues.

MIA LEVITIN is a cultural and literary critic whose work regularly appears in publications including the *Financial Times*, the *Irish Times* and *The Guardian*. She is the author of *The Future of Seduction*.

NATALIE BYRNE is an award-winning Latina illustrator and author based in London. She found her illustrative voice combining colour and important topics. Her work promotes intersectional feminism and tackles social issues such as sexual assault, mental health and equality, and she has worked with the BBC, Nike, Adobe, the Body Shop and many others. Her debut book, *Period*, is full of practical tips and advice on everything you need to know about periods. Natalie also illustrated the bestseller *Break the Mould*, written by Sinead Burke, and won Irish Children's Book of the Year 2020, in the senior category.

NICOLA SLAWSON is passionate about telling human stories – either other people's or her own – and is a freelance journalist, writer and public speaker. In her journalism work she writes mainly for *The Guardian* and Positive News, but her byline has also been seen in the *Sunday Telegraph*, *Evening Standard*, *The Observer*, *Psychologies* magazine and *HuffPost*, among others. Her personal essays have appeared in *Refinery29*, *the I* newspaper, *The Guardian*, metro.co.uk and *The Independent*. Nicola is also the founder of *The Single Supplement*, an award-winning and popular weekly newsletter exploring the highs and lows of being single. She has been described as 'the poster child for single women' by *NYT* bestselling author Katherine May.

POORNA BELL is an award-winning journalist and author of seventeen years, and the former Executive Editor and Global Lifestyle Head for *HuffPost*. She won *Stylist*'s Rising Star Award for 2019, *Red* magazine's Big Book Award for 2019, was named as one of *Marie Claire*'s top thirty women and is a *Balance* magazine top 100 Wellness personality. A judge for the Mind Media Awards, she has written for *Red*, *The Telegraph*, *The Times*, *Stylist*, *the i* newspaper, the BBC, *The Guardian* and *Grazia*. She is a published author of three non-fiction books: her debut book was the acclaimed *Chase the Rainbow*, which she followed up with her award-winning *In Search of Silence*. Her third book, *Stronger: Changing Everything I Knew About Women's Strength*, is published by Bluebird/Pan Macmillan. She is an experienced public speaker and a regular contributor to BBC Radio.

RACHEL THOMPSON is a journalist who specialises in reporting on sex, relationships and gender. She is the senior culture reporter at *Mashable* and has written for *The Sunday Times*, CNN, *Elle*, *The Telegraph* and *HuffPost*. She is also the host of the *History Becomes Her* podcast, which explores the inspiring stories behind women currently making history. Her first book, *Rough* (Square Peg, 2021), is a non-fiction work exploring non-consensual rough sex and consent.

RAHEL AKLILU was born to Eritrean parents in North London in 1997. She writes essays, features and profiles across music and culture, having written for publications such as *gal-dem*, *Dazed*, *The Independent*, *VICE* and *CRACK*. Having grown up with a passion for both music and writing – which included entering and winning local creative-writing competitions as well as performing poetry – it wasn't until a chance encounter at a festival in Croatia that she decided to venture into music journalism, aged twenty-one. For Rahel, the most important thing about writing is being able to share the remarkable stories of remarkable people and bring their work to wider audiences. She holds a law degree from the London School of Economics and Political Science.

REBECCA REID is an author of *Perfect Liars*, *Truth Hurts*, *Two Wrongs* and *The Will*, and the non-fiction *The Power of Rude*. She is the former Digital Editor of *Grazia* and a current contributor to *The Daily Telegraph*. She is a TV and radio regular, who has made multiple appearances on *Woman's Hour*, the *Today* Programme, Sky News, *Good Morning Britain* and *This Morning*. She lives in Islington and is on a one-woman mission to make Chardonnay cool again.

ROSE STOKES is a writer and columnist specialising in women's rights, health, the environment and politics. Her work has appeared in numerous national titles in the UK, including the BBC, *The Economist*, *The Guardian*, *Grazia*, *VICE*, *Refinery29*, *The Independent* and *The Telegraph* and she has a regular column in the *Metro*. She is passionate about helping women to understand their bodies and their minds and how to look after them. She advocates strongly for personal freedom, sexual and reproductive rights and equality.

ROSIE WILBY is an award-winning comedian, speaker and broadcaster who has appeared on BBC Radio 4 programmes including *Woman's Hour*, *Saturday Live* and *Four Thought* and in the short film *The Bride and Bride*. Her first book, *Is Monogamy Dead?*, was longlisted for the Polari First Book Prize 2018 and followed a trilogy of acclaimed solo shows investigating the psychology of love and relationships. Rosie's second book, *The Breakup Monologues*, is based on her podcast of the same name, which was nominated for a British Podcast Award 2020 and has been recommended by *Chortle*, *Psychologies*, *The Observer* and *Metro*.

About the Contributors

SALMA EL-WARDANY is a writer, poet, speaker and BBC radio presenter who performs internationally, has given two TEDx Talks, and partners with organisations and global brands to have the uncomfortable conversations we have ignored for so long. As a Muslim woman of colour, she has struggled against stereotypes and marginalisation – specifically how difficult womanhood is in a patriarchal world. Her work centres around female storytelling and the power of a woman's voice.

SHANI SILVER is a writer and the host of *A Single Serving Podcast*. Her work focuses on changing the negative narratives around being single, in an effort to improve the way that single life is experienced. Shani's work helps singles reframe the limiting societal messages they take in, which focus almost exclusively on dating, as if they aren't allowed to care about anything else. Single people are whole, valid beings, capable of living infinitely amazing lives. Relationships are wonderful and we deserve to have them, but Shani knows that we don't deserve to be miserable in the meantime.

SHAPARAK KHORSANDI's career has taken her to all corners of the globe. She has appeared on countless TV and radio shows, including *Live at the Apollo*, *Michael McIntyre's Comedy Roadshow*, *Mock the Week*, *8 Out of 10 Cats*, *Have I Got News for You*, *QI*, *Just a Minute* and other flagship Radio 4 programmes. She has received an honorary doctorate from Winchester University for her contribution to the arts, and recently received the prestigious James Joyce Award from Dublin University. Her screenwriting debut was for Sky's *Little Crackers* and she has recently been commissioned to write a drama script for BBC Television. She has published three books: the first was her memoir, *A Beginner's Guide to Acting English*, followed by her debut novel *Nina Is Not OK*; her third book, a middle-grade novel called *Kissing Emma*, was published in September 2021.

SHON FAYE is a writer based in Bristol and one of the UK's leading commentators on trans politics. Originally training as a solicitor

About the Contributors

before leaving the law for the arts, she has worked variously as a writer, presenter, editor, screenwriter and cabaret comedian, and in the charity sector with Amnesty International and Stonewall. Her first short film was exhibited at Tate Britain's *Queer British Art* exhibition throughout 2017, and in 2018 she hosted Amnesty International's *Women Making History* festival, held to celebrate the centenary of women's suffrage. She was an Editor-at-large at *Dazed*, and her writing has been published by *The Guardian*, *The Independent* and *VICE*, among others. Her first book, *The Transgender Issue*, was published by Penguin Press in 2021.

SOPHIA LEONIE is a writer, actress and former teacher. As a journalist and opinion writer, she focuses on issues of identity, relationships and popular culture and is a regular freelance writer for the online magazine *gal-dem*. As a cultural critic and artist, Sophia has spoken on a range of media platforms, including BBC Radio 1 and Channel 4 News. She is also a playwright and screenwriter, becoming one of the 2021 recipients of the Neal Street Productions screenwriters' bursary, and is currently writing her first full-length feature film.

SOPHIA MONEY-COUTTS is a journalist, author and *Sunday Telegraph* columnist who spends most of her time writing at her kitchen table. Prior to going freelance, she worked for various newspapers and magazines, including the *Evening Standard*, *Daily Mail* and *Tatler*, where she spent five particularly eccentric years studying the aristocracy. Her fourth novel, *Did You Miss Me?*, was published in 2020. She's been through more break-ups than Henry VIII and is very happily single.

STEPHANIE YEBOAH is a freelance writer, public speaker and fat-acceptance advocate, and a multi-award-nominated content creator. She has written her self-titled blog for more than twelve years and has also written extensively for publications including British *Vogue*, *Stylist* magazine, *Elle*, *GQ*, *The Guardian*, *The Independent* and *Who What Wear*, on body positivity, race, intersectional feminism and dating from the perspective of a black, plus-size woman living in the UK.

VENUS LIBIDO is an illustrator, sex educator and presenter best known for her strikingly honest and sometimes controversial drawings, and for her sex-positive chat show *Private Parts*. She dedicates her time to breaking down stigmas when it comes to self-pleasure and using sex toys, and talks openly about being pansexual. Venus has also shared her ongoing battle with endometriosis and how to have an enjoyable sex life, even with gynaecology issues.

Acknowledgements

This book may be called *Unattached*, but there are many people who are intrinsically attached to it, and without whom it would not have been possible. Like the pages in your hands, this book is made from a rich tapestry of support and advice from – and conversations with – an array of incredible women. To all the contributors, thank you so much for baring your souls in these pages. I hope your openness and honesty in writing about singlehood have paved the way for women to thrive and find joy in their lives, no matter what their relationship status.

To my publishing team, thank you for believing in this anthology from its inception. To my agent Florence Rees at A. M. Heath, you are a formidable force and have been a guiding presence in every step of publishing this book. I am indebted to the whole team at Square Peg, especially my editor Mireille Harper, for believing in me as a writer from our initial cinnamon-bun-fuelled meetings and for bringing such zest and energy to this project; and to her editorial assistant, Maxine Sibihwana, for her keen eye for detail.

To my best friends Gemma Perlin and Claude Levy, your support, kindness and empathy know no bounds, and there would not be this book without the lessons in love and friendship that you have taught me over the last ten years. You have shown me, through the million phone calls, cups of tea and late-night pep talks, that romantic love isn't always the answer – and that life opens up when you realise your friends can be your soulmates, too.

To my work-wife Rebecca Reid, thank you for your endless encouragement and career chats – our weekly Wednesday walks through Hampstead Heath were the highlight of my lockdown and